'The startling truth behind the veiled lives of Saudi
Arabia's women . . . frank and vivid revelations'
Sunday Express

'*Princess* is a mind-boggling look at the everyday
life of a contemporary woman in the
21,000-member-strong royal family . . . absolutely
riveting'
People Magazine

'Gripping . . . a fast-paced, enthralling drama
rich in detail . . . '
Publishers Weekly

'Anyone with the slightest interest in
human rights will find this book
heart-wrenching. It is a well-written,
personal story . . . It had to come from a
native woman to be believable'

Betty Mahmoody, bestselling author of
Not Without My Daughter

PRINCESS

Jean P. Sasson

BANTAM BOOKS

LONDON · NEW YORK · TORONTO · SYDNEY · AUCKLAND

PRINCESS
A BANTAM BOOK 0 553 40570 5

Originally published in Great Britain by Doubleday,
a division of Transworld Publishers Ltd

PRINTING HISTORY
Doubleday edition published 1992
Bantam books edition published 1993
Bantam Books edition reprinted 1993 (three times)

Set in 11/13pt Linotype Bembo by
Chippendale Type Ltd, Otley, West Yorkshire

Bantam Books are published by
Transworld Publishers Ltd,
61–63 Uxbridge Road, Ealing, London W5 5SA,
in Australia by
Transworld Publishers (Australia) Pty Ltd,
15–25 Helles Avenue, Moorebank, NSW 2170,
and in New Zealand by
Transworld Publishers (NZ) Ltd,
3 William Pickering Drive, Albany, Auckland.

Printed and bound in Great Britain by
Cox & Wyman Ltd, Reading, Berks.

This book is dedicated to

JACK W. CREECH

From the first moment, he believed in the importance of telling Sultana's story. He alone knows the anguish I endured in reliving my long friendship with Sultana in the writing of this book; and he, more than any other person, generously gave his friendship and emotional support during difficult times as this book slowly became a reality.

Contents

Acknowledgements

Once I was convinced that I should write this book, I read and reread Sultana's notes and diaries that she had entrusted to me. As I selected the adventures of her amazing life to portray in this book, I felt the excitement of a detective. Yet I was burdened with a solemn responsibility carefully to discard the events that would surely lead trouble to her door. The words are mine, but the story is hers.

Thank you, Sultana, for bravely sharing your life-story with the world. By taking this bold step, you have helped to humanize the Arabs, a people misunderstood by the West. My hope is that by revealing the intimate details of your life as an Arab woman, in all its pain and glory, your story will help to dispel the many negative stereotypes held of your people throughout the world. Readers of your story cannot help but understand that, as in any country of the world, there is good along with the bad. We of the West have heard only the bad of Saudi Arabia. I know, and you know, that, in spite of the primitive customs that cruelly bind females in your land, there are many Arabs, like you, who deserve our respect and admiration for their struggles against centuries of oppression.

Closer to home, I sincerely thank Liza Dawson, my editor at William Morrow, who fell in love with Sultana's story at her first reading of the manuscript. Her comments and suggestions further enhanced it.

Also, I want to thank Peter Miller, my literary agent. His energetic enthusiasm for this book never lagged and is appreciated.

Very special thanks are reserved for Pat L. Creech, PhD, who from the beginning assisted me with comments and editorial revisions. Her brilliance helped to shape this book.

I would have found writing Sultana's story much more difficult without the love and support of my family. I owe a special debt of gratitude to my parents, Neatwood and Mary Parks. Their ever-present love and support was even more deeply felt during the writing of this very personal book.

The story of Princess Sultana is true. While the words are those of the author, the story is that of the Princess. The shocking human tragedies described here are factual.

Names have been changed and various events slightly altered to protect the wellbeing of recognizable individuals.

In telling this true story it is not the intention of the author nor of the Princess to demean the Islamic faith.

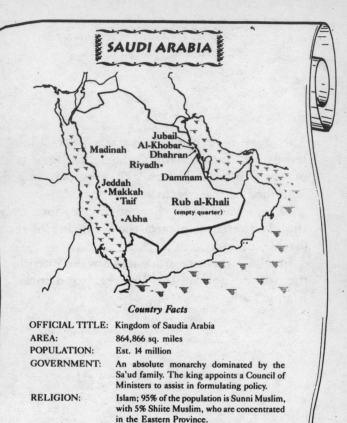

SAUDI ARABIA

Jubail
Al-Khobar
Madinah
Dhahran
Riyadh
Dammam
Jeddah
Makkah
Taif
Rub al-Khali
(empty quarter)
Abha

Country Facts

OFFICIAL TITLE: Kingdom of Saudia Arabia

AREA: 864,866 sq. miles

POPULATION: Est. 14 million

GOVERNMENT: An absolute monarchy dominated by the Sa'ud family. The king appoints a Council of Ministers to assist in formulating policy.

RELIGION: Islam; 95% of the population is Sunni Muslim, with 5% Shiite Muslim, who are concentrated in the Eastern Province.

LANGUAGES: Arabic. English is widely spoken in business circles.

CLIMATE: Hot and dry. Temperatures can reach 130°F in the hot summer months. During the winter months, the temperature varies between 50°F and 80°.

CURRENCY: Saudi Riyals. U.S. $1 = SR 3.73

ECONOMY: Wealth is based on petroleum exports. Saudi Arabia is the largest producer within OPEC. One sixth of the world's total of oil is produced in this country.

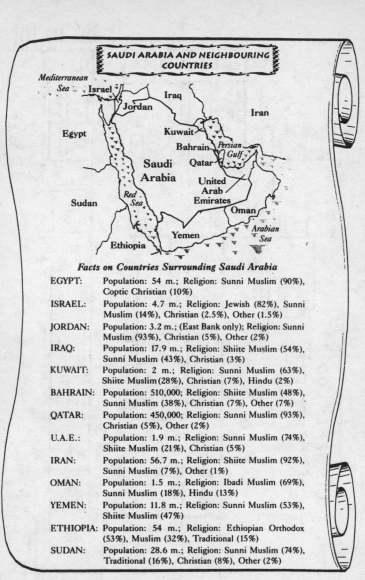

SAUDI ARABIA AND NEIGHBOURING COUNTRIES

Mediterranean Sea — Israel — Iraq — Iran — Jordan — Egypt — Kuwait — Bahrain — *Persian Gulf* — Saudi Arabia — Qatar — United Arab Emirates — Sudan — *Red Sea* — Oman — *Arabian Sea* — Ethiopia — Yemen

Facts on Countries Surrounding Saudi Arabia

EGYPT: Population: 54 m.; Religion: Sunni Muslim (90%), Coptic Christian (10%)

ISRAEL: Population: 4.7 m.; Religion: Jewish (82%), Sunni Muslim (14%), Christian (2.5%), Other (1.5%)

JORDAN: Population: 3.2 m.; (East Bank only); Religion: Sunni Muslim (93%), Christian (5%), Other (2%)

IRAQ: Population: 17.9 m.; Religion: Shiite Muslim (54%), Sunni Muslim (43%), Christian (3%)

KUWAIT: Population: 2 m.; Religion: Sunni Muslim (63%), Shiite Muslim (28%), Christian (7%), Hindu (2%)

BAHRAIN: Population: 510,000; Religion: Shiite Muslim (48%), Sunni Muslim (38%), Christian (7%), Other (7%)

QATAR: Population: 450,000; Religion: Sunni Muslim (93%), Christian (5%), Other (2%)

U.A.E.: Population: 1.9 m.; Religion: Sunni Muslim (74%), Shiite Muslim (21%), Christian (5%)

IRAN: Population: 56.7 m.; Religion: Shiite Muslim (92%), Sunni Muslim (7%), Other (1%)

OMAN: Population: 1.5 m.; Religion: Ibadi Muslim (69%), Sunni Muslim (18%), Hindu (13%)

YEMEN: Population: 11.8 m.; Religion: Sunni Muslim (53%), Shiite Muslim (47%)

ETHIOPIA: Population: 54 m.; Religion: Ethiopian Orthodox (53%), Muslim (32%), Traditional (15%)

SUDAN: Population: 28.6 m.; Religion: Sunni Muslim (74%), Traditional (16%), Christian (8%), Other (2%)

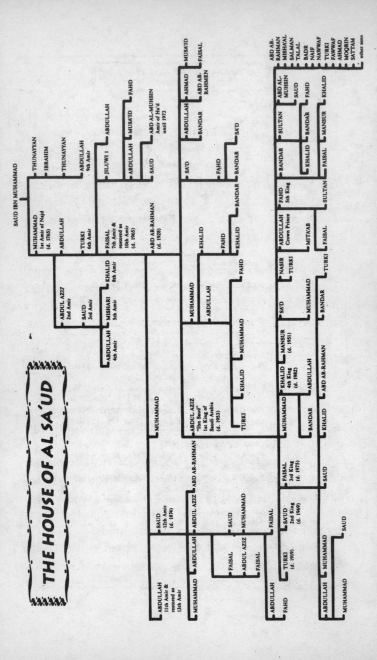

THE HOUSE OF AL SA'UD

Introduction

In a land where kings still rule, I am a princess. You must know me only as Sultana. I cannot reveal my true name for fear harm will come to me and my family for what I am about to tell you.

I am a Saudi princess, a member of the royal family of the House of Al Sa'ud, the current rulers of the Kingdom of Saudi Arabia. As a woman in a land ruled by men, I cannot speak directly to you. I have requested an American friend and writer, Jean Sasson, to listen to me and then to tell my story.

I was born free, yet today I am in chains. Invisible, they were loosely draped and passed unnoticed until the age of understanding reduced my life to a narrow segment of fear.

No memories are left to me of my first four years. I suppose I laughed and played as all young children do, blissfully unaware that my value, owing to the absence of a male organ, was of no significance in the land of my birth.

To understand my life, you must know those who came before me. We present-day Al Sa'uds date back six generations to the days of the early emirs of the Nadj, the bedouin lands now part of the Kingdom of Saudi Arabia. These first Al Sa'uds were men whose dreams carried them no farther than the conquest of nearby desert lands and the adventures of night raids on neighbouring tribes.

In 1891 disaster struck when the Al Sa'ud clan was defeated in battle and forced to flee the Nadj. Abdul Aziz, who would one day be my grandfather, was a child at this time. He barely survived the hardships of that desert flight. Later he would recall how he burned with shame as his father ordered him to crawl into a large bag which was then slung over the saddle horn of his camel. His sister, Nura, was cramped into another bag hanging from the other side of their father's camel. Bitter that his youth prevented him from fighting to save his home, the angry young man peered from the bag as he swayed with the gait of the camel. It was a turning-point in his young life, he would later recall, as he, humiliated by his family's defeat, watched the haunting beauty of his homeland disappear from view.

After two years of nomadic desert travel, the family of Al Sa'uds found refuge in the country of Kuwait. The life of a refugee was so distasteful to Abdul Aziz that he vowed from an early age to recapture the desert sands he had once called home.

So it was that in September 1901, twenty-five-year-old Abdul Aziz returned to our land. On 16 January 1902, after months of hardship, he and his men soundly defeated his enemies, the Rasheeds. In the years to follow, to ensure the loyalty of the desert tribes, Abdul Aziz married more than 300 women, who in time produced more than fifty sons and eighty daughters. The sons of his favourite wives held the honour of favoured status; these sons, now grown, are at the very centre of power in our land. No wife of Abdul Aziz was more loved than Hassa Sudairi. The sons of Hassa now head the combined forces of Al Sa'uds to rule the kingdom forged by their father. Fahd, one of these sons, is now our king.

Many sons and daughters married cousins of the prominent sections of our family such as the Al Turkis, Jiluwis and Al Kabirs. The present-day princes from these unions are among influential Al Sa'uds. In 1991 our extended family consisted of nearly 21,000 members. Of this number, approximately a thousand are princes or princesses who are direct descendants of the great leader, King Abdul Aziz.

I, Sultana, am one of these direct descendants.

My first vivid memory is one of violence. When I was four years old, I was slapped across the face by my usually gentle mother. Why? I had imitated my father in his prayers. Instead of praying to Makkah, I prayed to my six-year-old brother, Ali. I thought he was a god. How was I to know he was not? Thirty-two years later, I remember the sting of that slap and the beginning of questions in my mind: If my brother were not a god, why was he treated like one?

In a family of ten daughters and one son, fear ruled our home: fear that cruel death would claim the one living male child, fear that no other sons would follow, fear that God had cursed our home with daughters. My mother feared each pregnancy, praying for a son, dreading a daughter. She bore one daughter after another – until there were ten in all.

My mother's worst fear came true when my father took another, younger wife for the purpose of giving him more precious sons. The new wife of promise presented him with three sons, all stillborn, before he divorced her. Finally, though, with the fourth wife, my father became wealthy with sons. But my elder brother would always be the firstborn and, as such, he ruled supreme. Like my sisters, I pretended to revere my brother, but I hated him as only the oppressed can hate.

When my mother was twelve years old, she was married to my father. He was twenty. It was 1946, the year after the great world war that interrupted oil production had ended. Oil, the vital force of Saudi Arabia today, had not yet brought great wealth to my father's family, the Al Sa'uds, but its impact on the family was felt in small ways. The leaders of great nations had begun to pay homage to our king. The British prime minister, Winston Churchill, had presented King Abdul Aziz with a luxurious Rolls-Royce. Bright green, with a throne-like back seat, the car sparkled like a jewel in the sun. Something about the car, as grand as it was, obviously disappointed the king, for upon inspection he gave it to one of his favourite brothers, Abdullah.

Abdullah, who was my father's uncle and close friend, offered him this car for his honeymoon trip to Jeddah. He accepted, much to the delight of my mother, who had never ridden in a car. In 1946 – and dating back untold centuries – the camel was the usual mode of transport in the Middle East. Three decades would pass before the average Saudi rode with comfort in a car rather than astride a camel.

Now, on their honeymoon, for seven days and nights, my parents happily crossed the desert trail to Jeddah. Unfortunately, in my father's haste to depart from Riyadh, he had forgotten his tent; because of this oversight and the presence of several slaves, their marriage remained unconsummated until they arrived in Jeddah.

That dusty exhausting trip was one of my mother's happiest memories. Forever after, she divided her life into 'the time before the trip' and 'the time after the trip'. Once she told me that the trip had been the end of her youth, for she was too young to understand what lay ahead of her at the end of the long journey. Her parents had died in a fever epidemic, leaving her orphaned at the age of eight. She had been married at the age of twelve to an intense man filled with dark cruelties. She was ill-equipped to do little more in life than his bidding.

After a brief stay in Jeddah, my parents returned to Riyadh, for it was there that the patriarchal family of the Al Sa'uds continued their dynasty.

My father was a merciless man; as a predictable result, my mother was a melancholy woman. Their tragic union eventually produced sixteen children of whom eleven survived perilous childhoods. Today, their ten female offspring live their lives controlled by the men to whom they are married. Their only surviving son, a prominent Saudi prince and businessman with four wives and numerous mistresses, leads a life of great promise and pleasure.

From my reading, I know that most civilized successors of early cultures smile at the primitive ignorance of their ancestors. As civilization advances, the fear of freedom for the individual is overcome through enlightenment. Human society eagerly rushes to embrace knowledge and change. Astonishingly, the land of my ancestors is little changed from that of a thousand years ago. Yes, modern buildings spring up, the latest health care is available to all, but consideration for women and for the quality of their lives still receives a shrug of indifference.

It is wrong, however, to blame our Muslim faith for the lowly position of women in our society. Although the Koran does state that women are secondary to men, much in the same way the Bible authorizes men to rule over women, our Prophet Muhammad taught only kindness and fairness towards those of my sex. The men who came behind Prophet Muhammad have chosen to follow the customs and traditions of the Dark Ages rather than to follow Muhammad's words and example. Our Prophet scorned the practice of infanticide, a common custom in his day of ridding the family of unwanted females. Prophet Muhammad's very words ring with his concern at the possibility of abuse and indifference towards females: 'Whoever hath a daughter, and doth not bury her alive, or scold her, or prefer his male children to her, may God bring him into Paradise.'

Yet there is nothing men will not do, there is nothing they have not done, in this land to ensure the birth of male, not female, offspring. The worth of a child born in the Kingdom of Saudi Arabia is still measured by the absence or the presence of a male organ.

The men of my country feel they are what they have had to become. In Saudi Arabia, the pride of a man's honour evolves from his women, so he must enforce his authority and supervision over the sexuality of his women or face public disgrace. Convinced that women have no control over their own sexual desires, it then becomes essential that the dominant male carefully guard the sexuality of the female. This absolute control over the female has nothing to do with love, only with fear of the male's tarnished honour.

The authority of a Saudi male is unlimited; his wife and children survive only if he desires. In our homes, he is the state. This complex situation begins with the rearing of our young boys. From an early age, the male child is taught that women are of little value: they exist only for his comfort and convenience. The child witnesses the disdain shown for his mother and sisters by his father; this open contempt leads to his scorn of all females, and makes it impossible for him to enjoy friendship with anyone of the opposite sex. Taught only the role of master to slave, it is little wonder that by the time he is old enough to take a mate he considers her his chattel, not his partner.

And so it comes to be that women in my land are ignored by their fathers, scorned by their brothers and abused by their husbands. This cycle is difficult to break, for the men who impose this life upon their women ensure their own marital unhappiness. For what man can be truly content surrounded by such misery? It is evident that the men of my land are searching for gratification by taking one wife after the other, followed by mistress after mistress. Little do these men know that their happiness can be found in their own home, with one woman of equality. By treating women as slaves, as property, men have made themselves as unhappy as the women they rule, and have made love and true companionship unattainable to both sexes.

The history of our women is buried behind the black veil of secrecy. Neither our birth nor our death is made official in any public record. Although births of male children are documented in family or tribal records, none is maintained anywhere for females. The common emotion expressed at the birth of a female is either sorrow or shame. Although hospital births and government record-keeping are increasing, the majority of rural births take place at home. No country census is maintained by the government of Saudi Arabia.

I have often asked myself: Does this mean that we women of the desert do not exist, if our coming and our passing go unrecorded? If no-one knows of my existence, does that mean I do not exist?

This fact, more than the injustices of my life, have prompted me to take this very real risk in order to tell my story. The women of my country may be hidden by the veil and firmly controlled by our stern patriarchal society, but change will have to come, for we are a sex that is weary of the restraints of customs. We yearn for our personal freedom.

From my earliest memories, aided by the secret diary I began to keep at the age of eleven, I will try to give you some portrayal of the life of a princess in the House of Al Sa'ud. I will attempt to uncover the buried lives of other Saudi women, the millions of ordinary women not born of the royal family.

My passion for the truth is simple, for I am one of those women who were ignored by their father, scorned by their brother, and abused by their husband. I am not alone in this. There are many more, just like me, who have no opportunity to tell their stories.

It is rare that truth escapes from a Saudi palace, for there is great secrecy in our society, but what I have spoken here and what the author has written here is true.

Chapter One

Childhood

Ali slapped me to the ground, but I declined to hand over the shiny red apple just given to me by the Pakistani cook. Ali's face began to swell with anger as I hovered over the apple and quickly began to take huge bites and swallow them whole. Refusing to give in to his male prerogative of superiority, I had committed a grave act and knew that I would soon suffer the consequences. Ali gave me two swift kicks and went running for our father's driver, Omar, an Egyptian. My sisters feared Omar almost as much as they did Ali or my father. They disappeared into the villa, leaving me alone to face the combined wrath of the men of the house.

Moments later, Omar, followed by Ali, rushed through the side-gate. I knew they would be the victors, for my young life was already rich with precedent. I had learned at an early age that Ali's every wish would be fulfilled. Nevertheless, I swallowed the last bite of the apple and looked in triumph at my brother.

Struggling vainly in the grasp of Omar's huge hands, I was lifted into the air and transported to my father's study. Reluctantly, my father looked up from his black ledger and glanced with irritation at his seemingly ever-present unwanted daughter while holding out his arms in invitation to that treasured jewel, his eldest son.

Ali was allowed to speak, while I was forbidden to respond. Overwhelmed with desire for my father's love and approval, my courage was suddenly reborn. I shouted out the truth of the incident. My father and brother were stunned into silence at my outburst, for females in my world are reconciled to a stern society that frowns upon the voicing of our opinions. All women learn at an early age to manipulate rather than to confront. The fires in the hearts of the once proud and fierce bedouin women have been extinguished; soft women who bear little resemblance to them remain in their stead.

The fear curled in my belly when I heard the shouting of my voice. My legs trembled under my body when my father arose from his chair, and I saw the movement of his arm but never felt the blow to my face.

As punishment, Ali was given all my toys. To teach me that men were my masters, my father decreed that Ali would have the exclusive right to fill my plate at mealtimes. The triumphant Ali gave me the tiniest of portions and the worst cuts of meat. Each night, I went to sleep hungry, for Ali placed a guard at my door and ordered him to forbid me to receive food from my mother or my sisters. My brother taunted me by entering my room at midnight laden with plates steaming with the delicious smells of cooked chicken and hot rice.

Finally Ali wearied of his torture, but from that time on, when he was only nine years old, he was my devoted enemy. Although I was only seven years old, as a result of the apple incident I first became aware that I was a female who was shackled by males unburdened by consciences. I saw the broken spirits of my mother and sisters, but I remained faithful to optimism and never doubted that I would one day triumph and my pain would be compensated by true justice. With this determination, from an early age, I was the family troublemaker.

There were pleasant times in my young life, too. My happiest hours were spent at the home of my mother's aunt. Widowed, too old for further notice and thus complications from men, she was now merry and filled with wonderful stories from her youth of the days of the tribal battles. She had witnessed the birth of our nation and mesmerized us with the tales of the valour of King Abdul Aziz and his followers. Sitting cross-legged on priceless oriental carpets, my sisters and I nibbled on plates of date pastries and almond cakes while immersed in the drama of the great victories of our kinsmen. My aunty inspired me to new pride in my family as she told of the Al Sa'uds' bravery in battle.

In 1891 my mother's family had accompanied the Al Sa'ud clan in their flight from Riyadh when they were defeated by the Rasheed clan. Ten years later, male members of her family returned with

27

Abdul Aziz to recapture the land; my aunty's brother fought alongside Abdul Aziz. This show of loyalty ensured their entry into the royal family by the marriage of their daughters. The stage was set for my destiny as a princess.

In my youth, my family was privileged, though not yet wealthy. The income from oil production ensured that food was plentiful and medical care available, which at that time in our history seemed the greatest of luxuries.

We lived in a large villa made of concrete blocks painted snowy white. Each year, the sandstorms turned the white to cream, but father's slaves would dutifully repaint the sand-coloured stones white. The thirty-foot block walls surrounding our grounds were maintained in the same fashion. The childhood home I took for granted was a mansion by Western standards; yet, looking back, it was a simple dwelling by today's Saudi royal expectations.

As a child, I felt our family home was too large for warm comfort. The long hallways were dark and forbidding. Rooms of various shapes and sizes branched off, concealing the secrets of our lives. Father and Ali lived in the men's quarters on the second floor. I used to peer into their quarters with the curiosity of the child I was. Dark-red velvet curtains closed out the sunlight. A smell of Turkish tobacco and whisky embraced the heavy atmosphere. One timid look and then with a rush I would return to the women's quarters on the ground floor, where my sisters and I

28

occupied a large wing. The room I shared with Sara faced the women's private garden. Mother had had the room painted a bright yellow; as a result, it had the glow of life that was so glaringly absent in the rest of the villa.

The family servants and slaves lived in tiny airless rooms in a separate dwelling set apart at the back of the garden. While our villa was air-conditioned, the servants' quarters were ill-equipped for enduring the hot desert climate. I remember the foreign maids and drivers speaking of their dread of bedtime. Their only relief from the heat was the breeze generated by small electric fans. Father said that if he provided their quarters with air-conditioning they would sleep the whole day through.

Only Omar slept in a small room in the main house. A long golden cord hung in the main entrance of our villa. This cord was connected to a cowbell in Omar's room. When Omar was needed, he would be summoned by the ringing of this bell; the sound of the bell, day or night, would bring him to his feet and to Father's door. Many times, I must admit, I rang the bell during Omar's naps, or in the middle of the night. Then, lungs bursting, I would rush to my bed and lie quiet, an innocent child sleeping soundly. One night my mother was waiting for me as I raced for the bed. With disappointment etched on her face at the misdeeds of her youngest child, she twisted my ear and threatened to tell Father. But she never did.

Since my grandfather's day, we had owned a family of Sudanese slaves. Our slave population increased each year when Father returned from Haj, the annual pilgrimage to Makkah made by Muslims, with new slave children. Pilgrims from Sudan and Nigeria, attending Haj, would sell their children to wealthy Saudis so that they could afford the return journey to their homeland. Once in my father's care, the slaves were not bought and sold in the manner of the American slaves; they participated in our home life and in my father's businesses as if they were their own. The children were our playmates and felt no compulsion to servitude. In 1962, when our government freed the slaves, our Sudanese family actually cried and begged my father to keep them. They live in my father's home to this day.

My father kept alive the memory of our beloved king, Abdul Aziz. He spoke about the great man as if he saw him each day. I was shocked, at the age of eight, to be told the old king had died in 1953, three years before I was born!

After the death of our first king, our kingdom was in grave danger, for the old king's hand-picked successor, his son Sa'ud, was sadly lacking in qualities of leadership. He extravagantly squandered most of the country's oil wealth on palaces, cars, and trinkets for his wives. As a result, our new country was sliding towards political and economic chaos.

I recall one occasion in 1963 when the men of the ruling family gathered in our home. I was a very curious seven-year-old at the time. Omar, my father's driver, burst into the garden with a manner of great importance and shouted for the women to go upstairs. He waved his hands at us as if he were exorcizing the house of beasts and literally herded us up the stairwell and into a small sitting-room. Sara, my older sister, pleaded with my mother for permission to hide behind the arabesque balcony for a rare glimpse of our rulers at work. While we frequently saw our powerful male uncles and cousins at casual family gatherings, never were we present in the midst of important matters of state. Of course, at the time of each female's menses and subsequent veiling, the cut-off from any males other than father and brothers was sudden and complete.

Our lives were so cloistered and boring that even our mother took pity on us. That day, she actually joined her daughters on the floor of the hallway to peep through the balcony and listen to the men in the large sitting-room below us. I, as the youngest, was held in my mother's lap. As a precaution, she lightly placed her fingers on my lips. If we were caught, my father would be furious.

My sisters and I were captivated by the grand parade of the sons, grandsons and nephews of the deceased king. Large men in flowing robes, they gathered quietly with great dignity and seriousness. The stoic face of Crown Prince Faisal drew our attention. Even to my young eyes, he appeared sad and terribly burdened. By 1963 all Saudis were aware that Prince Faisal competently managed the country while King Sa'ud ruled incompetently. It was whispered that Sa'ud's reign was only a symbol of the family unity so fiercely protected. The feeling was that it was an odd arrangement, unfair to the country and to Prince Faisal, and unlikely to last.

Prince Faisal stood apart from the group. His usual quiet voice rose above the din as he asked that he be allowed to speak on matters that were of grave importance to the family and the country. Prince Faisal feared that the throne which had been so difficult to attain would soon be lost. He said that the common people were tiring of the excesses of the royal family, and that there was talk not only of ousting their brother Sa'ud for his decadence, but also of turning away from the entire Al Sa'ud clan and choosing instead a man of God for leadership.

Prince Faisal looked hard at the younger princes when he stated in a clear, sure voice that their disregard for the traditional lifestyle of bedouin believers would topple the throne. He said his heart was heavy from sadness that so few of the younger royals were willing to work, content to live on their monthly stipend from the oil wealth. A long pause ensued as he waited for comments from his brothers and relatives. As none seemed to be forthcoming, he added that if he, Faisal, were at the controls of the oil wealth, the flow of money to the princes would be cut and honourable work would be sought. He nodded his head at his brother Muhammad and sat down with a sigh. From the balcony, I noticed the nervous squirming of several youthful cousins. Even though the largest monthly stipend was no more than ten thousand dollars, the men of the Al Sa'ud clan grew increasingly wealthy from the land. Saudi Arabia is a huge country, and most of the property belongs to our family. In addition, no building contracts are signed without benefit to one of our own.

Prince Muhammad, the third-eldest living brother, began to speak; and, from what we could gather, King Sa'ud had now insisted on the return of absolute power that had been taken from him in 1958. He was rumoured to be in the countryside, speaking out against his brother Faisal. It was a devastating moment for the family of Al Sa'ud, for its members had always shown a unified front to the citizens of Saudi Arabia.

I remember when my father had told the story of why the eldest living son after Faisal, Muhammad, was passed over as successor to the throne. The old king had declared that if Muhammad's disposition were backed by the power of the Crown many men would die, for Muhammad's violent temper was well known.

My attention returned to the meeting, and I heard Prince Muhammad say that the monarchy itself was endangered; he broached the possibility of physically overthrowing the king and installing Prince Faisal in his stead. Prince Faisal gasped so loudly that the sound stifled Muhammad. Faisal seemed to be weeping as he spoke quietly. He told his kin that he had given his beloved father a deathbed promise that he would never oppose the rule of his brother. In no event would he consider breaking the promise, not even if Sa'ud bankrupted the country. If talk of ousting his brother was going to be the heart of the meeting, then he, Faisal, would have to depart.

There was a hum of voices as the men of our family agreed that Muhammad, the eldest brother next to Faisal, should attempt to reason with our king. We watched as the men toyed with their coffee-cups and made vows of loyalty to their father's wish that all the sons of Abdul Aziz would confront the world as a united force. As the traditional exchange of farewells began, we watched as the men filed as silently from the room as they had entered.

Little did I know that this meeting was the beginning of the end of the rule of my uncle, King Sa'ud. As history unfolded, and our family and countrymen watched in sadness, the sons of Abdul Aziz were forced to evict one of their own from his land. Uncle Sa'ud had become so desperate that in the end he had sent a threatening note to his brother Prince Faisal. This one act sealed his fate, for it was unthinkable for one brother to insult or threaten another. In the unwritten rule of the bedouin, one brother never turns against the other.

A fevered crisis erupted within the family and the country. But we learned later that a revolution, sought by Uncle Sa'ud, had been averted by the soft approach of Crown Prince Faisal. He stepped aside and left it to his brothers and the men of religion to decide the best course of action for our young country. In doing so, he took away the personal drama of the movement so that it became a less volatile matter, with statesmen making appropriate decisions.

Two days later, we learned about the abdication from one of Uncle Sa'ud's wives, for our father had been away at the time with his brothers and cousins. One of our favourite aunties, married to King Sa'ud, burst into our home in great agitation. I was shocked to see her rip her veil from her face in front of our male servants. She had arrived from Uncle Sa'ud's Nasiriyah Palace (an edifice that, to my mind, was both a demonstration of what endless money can buy and a ruinous example of what was wrong with our country).

My sisters and I gathered around our mother, for our aunty was now out of control and screaming accusations about the family. She was particularly incensed at Crown Prince Faisal and blamed him for her husband's dilemma. She told us that the brothers of her husband had conspired to take the throne that had been given by their father to the one of his choice, Sa'ud. She cried out that the religious council, the Ulema, had arrived at the palace that very morning and had informed her husband that he must step aside as king.

I was entranced by the scene before me, for rarely do we view confrontation in our society. It is our nature to speak softly and agree with those before us and then to handle difficulties in a secret manner. When our aunty, who was a very beautiful woman with long black curls, began to tear out her hair and rip her expensive pearls from

35

her neck, I knew this was a serious matter. Finally my mother calmed her enough to lead her to the sitting-room for a cup of soothing tea. My sisters gathered around the closed door and tried to hear their whispering. I kicked around the large clumps of hair with my toe and stooped to gather the large smooth pearls. I found myself with fistfuls of pearls and placed them in an empty vase in the hallway for safe-keeping.

Mother guided our weeping aunty to her waiting black Mercedes. We all watched as the driver sped away with his inconsolable passenger. We never saw our aunty again, for she accompanied Uncle Sa'ud and his entourage into exile. But our mother did advise us against feeling harsh towards our Uncle Faisal. She said that our aunty had uttered such words because she was in love with a kind and generous man, but such a man does not necessarily make the best ruler. She told us that Uncle Faisal was leading our country into a stable and prosperous era, and by doing so he earned the wrath of those less capable. Although by Western standards my mother was uneducated, she was truly wise.

Chapter Two

Family

My mother, encouraged by King Faisal's wife Iffat, managed to educate her daughters, despite my father's resistance. For many years, my father refused even to consider the possibility. My five older sisters received no schooling other than to memorize the Koran from a private tutor who came to our home. For two hours, six afternoons a week, they would repeat words after the Egyptian teacher, Fatima, a stern woman of about forty-five years of age. She once asked my parents' permission to expand my sisters' education to include science, history and maths. Father responded with a firm no; and the recital of the Prophet's words, and his words alone, continued to ring throughout our villa.

As the years passed, Father saw that many of the royal families were allowing their daughters the benefit of an education. With the coming of the great oil wealth, which relieved nearly all Saudi women, other than the bedouin tribespeople and rural villagers, from any type of work, inactivity and boredom became a national problem. Members of the royal family are much wealthier than most Saudis, yet the oil wealth brought servants from the

Far East and other poor regions into every home.

All children need to be stimulated, but my sisters and I had little or nothing to do other than to play in our rooms or lounge in the women's gardens. There was nowhere to go and little to do, for when I was a child there was not even a zoo or a park in the city.

Mother, weary of five energetic daughters, thought that school would relieve her while expanding our minds. Finally Mother, with the assistance of Aunty Iffat, wore Father down to weak acceptance. And so it came to be that the five youngest daughters of our family, including Sara and myself, enjoyed the new age of reluctant acceptance of education for females.

Our first classroom was in the home of a royal relative. Seven families of the Al Sa'ud clan employed a young woman from Abu Dhabi, a neighbouring Arab city in the Emirates. Our small group of pupils, sixteen in all, was known in those days as a *kutab*, a group method then popular for teaching girls. We gathered daily in the home of our royal cousin from nine o'clock in the morning until two o'clock in the afternoon, Saturday to Thursday.

It was there that my favourite sister, Sara, first displayed her brilliance. She was much quicker than girls twice her age. The teacher even asked Sara if she was a primary graduate, and shook her head in wonder when she learned that Sara was not.

Our instructor had been fortunate to have a

modern-thinking father who had sent her to England for an education. Because of her deformity, a club foot, she had found no-one who would marry her, so she chose a path of freedom and independence for herself. She smiled as she told us that her deformed foot was a gift from God to ensure that her mind did not become deformed, too. Even though she lived in the home of our royal cousin (it was and still is unthinkable for a single woman to live alone in Saudi Arabia), she earned a salary and made her decisions about life without outside influence.

I liked her simply because she was kind and patient when I forgot to do my lessons. Unlike Sara, I was not the scholarly type, and I was happy the teacher expressed little disappointment at my shortcomings. I was much more interested in drawing than in maths, and in singing than in performing my prayers. Sara sometimes pinched me when I misbehaved, but after I howled in distress and disrupted the whole class, she left me to my mischievous ways. Certainly the instructor truly lived up to the name given her twenty-seven years before – Sakeena, which means 'tranquillity' in Arabic.

Miss Sakeena told Mother that Sara was the brightest student she had ever taught. After I jumped up and down and yelled, 'What about me?' she thought for a long moment before answering. With a smile, she said: 'And Sultana is certain to be famous.'

That evening at dinner, Mother proudly passed

on the remark about Sara to Father. Father, who was visibly pleased, smiled at Sara. Mother beamed with pleasure, but then Father cruelly asked how any daughter born of her belly could acquire learning. Nor did he credit Mother with any contribution to the brilliance of Ali, who was at the top of his class at a modern secondary school in the city. Presumably the intellectual achievements of her children were inherited solely from their father.

Even today I shudder with dismay while watching my older sisters attempt to add or subtract. I say little prayers of gratitude to Aunty Iffat, for she changed the lives of so many Saudi women.

In the summer of 1932, Uncle Faisal had travelled to Turkey and, while there, he had fallen in love with a unique young woman named Iffat al Thunayan. Hearing that the young Saudi prince was visiting Constantinople, the young Iffat and her mother approached him about disputed property that had belonged to her deceased father. (The Thunayans were originally Saudis but had been taken to Turkey by the Ottomans during their lengthy rule of the area.) Smitten by Iffat's beauty, Faisal invited her and her mother to Saudi Arabia to sort out the misunderstanding of the property matter. Not only did he give her the property; he also married her. Later he was to say it was the wisest decision of his life. My mother said Uncle Faisal had gone from woman to woman, like a man possessed, until he met Iffat.

During the years of Uncle Faisal's reign, Iffat became the driving force behind education for young girls. Without her efforts, the women in Arabia today would not be allowed in a classroom. I was in awe of her forceful character and declared I would grow up to be just like her. She even had the courage to hire an English nanny for her children who, of all the royal brood, turned out to be the most unaffected by great wealth.

Sadly, many of the royal cousins were swept away by the sudden rush of riches. My mother used to say that the bedouin had survived the stark emptiness of the desert but we would never survive the enormous wealth of the oilfields. The quiet achievements of the mind and the pious religious beliefs of their fathers hold no appeal for the vast majority of the younger Al Sa'uds. I believe that the children of this generation have decayed with the ease of their lives, and that their great fortune has deprived them of any ambitions or real satisfactions. Surely the weakness of our monarchy in Saudi Arabia is bound up in our addiction to extravagance. I fear it will be our undoing.

Most of my childhood was spent travelling from one city to another in my land. The nomadic bedouin blood flows in all Saudis, and as soon as we returned from one trip discussions would ensue as to the next journey. We Saudis no longer have sheep to graze, but we cannot stop looking for greener pastures.

Riyadh was the base of the Government, but none of the Al Sa'ud family particularly enjoyed the city; their complaints never ended about the dreariness of life in Riyadh. It was too hot and dry, the men of religion took themselves too seriously, the nights were too cold. Most of the family preferred Jeddah or Taif. Jeddah, with its ancient ports, was more open to change and moderation. There, we all breathed easier in the air of the sea.

We generally spent the months from December to February in Jeddah. We would return to Riyadh for March, April and May. The heat of the summer months would drive us to the mountains of Taif from June to September. Then it was back to Riyadh for October and November. Of course, we spent the month of Ramadan and two weeks of Haj in Makkah, our holy city.

By the time I was twelve years old, in 1968, my father had become extremely wealthy. In spite of his wealth, he was one of the least extravagant Al Sa'uds. But he did build each of his four families four palaces, in Riyadh, Jeddah, Taif and Spain. The palaces were exactly the same in each city, even to the colour of carpets and furniture selected. My father hated change, and he wanted to feel as if he were in the same home even after a flight from city to city. I remember him telling my mother to purchase four each of every item, down to the children's underwear. He did not want the family to bother with packing suitcases. I found it eerie that when I entered my room in Jeddah or Taif it was the same as my room in Riyadh, with the identical clothes hanging in identical wardrobes. My books and toys were purchased in fours, one of each item placed in each palace.

My mother rarely complained, but when my

father purchased four identical red Porsches for my brother, Ali, who was only fourteen at the time, she cried out that it was a shame – such waste – with so many poor in the world. When it came to Ali, though, no expense was spared.

When he was ten years old, Ali received his first gold Rolex watch. I was particularly distressed, for I had asked my father for a thick gold bracelet from the *souq* (market-place) and he had brusquely turned aside my request. During the second week of Ali flaunting his Rolex, I saw that he had laid it on the table beside the pool. Overcome with jealousy, I took a rock and pounded the watch to pieces.

For once, my mischief was not discovered, and it was with great pleasure that I saw my father reprimand Ali for being careless with his belongings. But of course, within a week or so, Ali was given another gold Rolex watch and my childish resentfulness returned with a vengeance.

My mother spoke to me often about my hatred for my brother. A wise woman, she saw the fire in my eye even as I bowed to the inevitable. As the youngest child of the family, I had been the most pampered of the daughters by my mother, sisters and other relatives. Looking back, it is hard to deny that I was spoiled beyond belief. Because I was small for my age, in contrast with the rest of my sisters, who were tall with large frames, I was treated as a baby throughout my childhood years. All of my sisters were quiet and restrained, as befitting Saudi princesses. I was loud and unruly, caring little for my royal image. How I must have tried their patience! But even today each of my sisters would spring to my defence at the first sign of danger.

In sad contrast, to my father I represented the last of many disappointments. As a consequence, I spent my childhood trying to win his affection. Finally, I despaired of attaining his love and clamoured after any attention, even if it were in the form of punishment for misdeeds. I calculated that if my father looked at me enough times he would recognize my special traits and come to love his daughter, even as he loved Ali. As it turned out, my rowdy ways ensured that he would go from indifference to open dislike.

My mother accepted the fact that the land in which we had been born was a place that is destined for misunderstandings between the sexes. Still a child, with the world stretching before me, I had yet to reach that conclusion.

Looking back, I suppose Ali must have had good character traits along with the bad, but it was difficult for me to see past his one great defect: Ali was cruel. I watched him as he taunted the handicapped son of our gardener. The poor child had long arms and strangely shaped legs. Often, when Ali's boyhood friends came over for a visit, he would summon poor Sami and tell him to do his 'monkey walk'. Ali never noticed the pathetic look on Sami's face or the tears that trickled down his cheeks.

When Ali found baby kittens, he would lock

them away from their mother and howl with glee as the mother cat tried in vain to reach them. No-one in the household dared to chastise Ali, for our father saw no harm in Ali's cruel ways.

After a particularly moving talk from my mother, I prayed about my feelings for Ali and decided to attempt the 'Saudi' way of manipulation instead of confrontation with my brother. Besides, my mother used God's wishes as her platform, and using God is always an admirable formula for convincing children to change their actions. Through my mother's eyes, I finally saw that my present course would lead me down a thorny path.

My good intentions were squashed within the week by Ali's dastardly behaviour. My sisters and I found a tiny puppy that had evidently become separated from its mother. The puppy was whimpering from hunger. Overcome with excitement at our find, we rushed about collecting dolls' bottles and warming goat's milk. My sisters and I took turns with feedings. Within days, the puppy was bouncing and fat. We dressed him in rags and even trained him to sit in our pram.

While it is true that Muslims do not favour dogs, it is a rare person who can harm a baby animal of any species. Even our mother, a devout Muslim, smiled at the antics of the puppy.

One afternoon we were pushing Basem, which means 'smiling face' in Arabic, in a pram. Ali happened to walk by with his friends. Sensing his friends' excitement over our puppy, Ali decided that the puppy should be his. My sisters and I screamed and fought when he tried to take Basem from our arms. Our father heard the commotion, and he came from his study. When Ali told him that he wanted the puppy, our father instructed us to hand him over. Nothing we said or did would change our father's mind. Ali wanted the puppy; Ali got the puppy.

Tears streamed down our faces as Ali jauntily walked away with Basem tucked under his arms. The possibility for love of my brother was forever lost, and my hate solidified when I was told that Ali had soon tired of Basem's whimpers and, on the way to visit friends, had tossed the puppy out of the window of the moving car.

Chapter Three

My Sister Sara

I felt wretched, for my favourite sister, Sara, was crying in Mother's arms. She is the ninth living daughter of my parents, three years older than I. Only Ali's birth separates us. It was Sara's sixteenth birthday, and she should have been rejoicing, but Mother had just relayed distressing news from Father.

Sara had been veiling since her menses, two years earlier. The veil stamped her as a non-person, and she soon ceased to speak of her childhood dreams of great accomplishment. She became distant from me, her younger sister who was as yet unconcerned with the institution of veiling. I was left longing for the remembered happiness of our shared childhood. It suddenly became apparent to me that happiness is realized only in the face of unhappiness, for I never knew we were so happy until Sara's unhappiness stared me in the face.

Sara was lovely, much more beautiful than I or my sisters. Her great beauty had become a curse, for many men had heard of Sara's beauty through their mothers and sisters and now wished to marry her. Sara was tall and slim, and her skin creamy and white. Her huge brown eyes sparkled with the knowledge that all who saw her admired her beauty. Her long black hair was the envy of all her sisters.

In spite of her natural beauty, Sara was genuinely sweet and loved by all who knew her. Unfortunately, not only did Sara acquire the curse that comes with great beauty; she was also exceptionally bright. In our land, brilliance in a woman assures her future misery, for there is nowhere to focus her genius.

Sara wanted to study art in Italy and be the first to open an art gallery in Jeddah. She had been working towards that goal since she was twelve years old. Her room was cluttered with books of all the great masters. Sara made my head swim with descriptions of the magnificent art in Europe. Just before the wedding announcement, when I was secretly plundering through her room, I saw a list of the places she planned to visit in Florence, Venice and Milan.

Sadly, I knew that Sara's dreams would not come true. While it is true that most marriages in my land are guided by the hands of the older females of the families, in our family Father was the decision-maker in all matters. Long ago, he had decided that his most beautiful daughter would marry a man of great prominence and wealth.

Now, the particular man he had chosen to marry his most desirable daughter was a member of a leading merchant family in Jeddah that had decided financial influence with our family. The groom was chosen solely because of past and future business deals. He was sixty-two years old; Sara would be his third wife. Although she had never met the old man, he had heard of her great beauty from his female relatives and was eager for the wedding date to be set. Mother had tried to intervene on Sara's behalf; but Father, as was his way, responded without emotion to his daughter's tears.

And now Sara had heard she was to wed. Mother ordered me to leave the room, but her back was turned; I tricked her by making noises with my feet and slamming the door. I slid inside the open wardrobe door and wept silent tears as my sister cursed our father, our land, our culture. She cried so hard that I lost many of her words, but I heard her cry out that she was sure to be sacrificed like a lamb.

My mother wept, too, but she had no words of comfort for Sara, for she knew her husband had the full right to dispose of their daughters in any marriage he liked. Six of their ten daughters were already married to men not of their choosing. Mother understood that the four remaining daughters would follow that darkness; there was no power on earth that could stop it.

Mother heard my squirming in the wardrobe. She narrowed her eyes and shook her head when she saw me, but made no effort to make me move. She told me to bring cold towels, and then she turned her attention back to Sara. When I returned, she placed the towels on Sara's head and soothed her to sleep. She sat and watched her young daughter for many minutes, and finally she rose wearily to her feet. With a long sad sigh, she took me by the hand and led me to the kitchen. Although it was not mealtime, and the cook was napping, Mother prepared for me a plate of cake and a glass of cold milk. I was thirteen, but small for my age; she cuddled me in her lap for a long time.

Unfortunately, Sara's tears served only to harden Father's heart. I overheard her entreaties to him. She became so unbalanced in her grief that she accused our father of hating women. She spat out a verse of Buddha: 'Victory breeds hatred, for the conquered are unhappy.' Father, his back rigid with anger, turned and walked away. Sara wailed at his back that she would have been better off unborn, since her pain so overweighed her happiness. With an ugly voice, Father responded by saying that her wedding date would be moved up to avoid stretching out her pain of anticipation.

Father normally came to our villa once every fourth night. Men of the Muslim faith, with four wives, rotate their evenings so that each wife and family is given an equal amount of time. It is a serious situation when a man refuses to go to his wife and children, a form of punishment. Our villa was in such an uproar with Sara's suffering that Father instructed Mother, who was his first and therefore his head wife, to inform his other three wives that he would rotate among their villas, but not ours. Before he left the villa, Father curtly told Mother to cure her daughter of her fever-ish resentments and to guide her peacefully to her destiny, which in his words was that of a 'dutiful wife and good mother'.

I barely recall the weddings of my other sisters. I vaguely remember tears, but I was so young and the emotional trauma of marriage to a stranger had not yet penetrated my thoughts. But I can close my eyes today and bring to mind every detail of the events that occurred in the months before Sara's wedding, the wedding itself, and the sad events that unfolded in the weeks afterwards.

I held the family reputation of the difficult child, the daughter who most tried my parents' patience. Wilful and reckless, I created havoc in our household. I was the one who poured sand into the motor of Ali's new Mercedes; I pinched money out of my father's wallet; I buried Ali's gold coin collection in the backyard; I released green snakes and ugly lizards from jars into the family pool as Ali lay sleeping on his float.

Sara was the perfect daughter, with her quiet obedience, and had earned perfect marks for her schoolwork. Even though I loved her madly, I thought Sara weak. But she surprised us all during the weeks prior to her wedding. Apparently she had hidden strength, for she called our father's office daily and left messages for him that she was not going to marry. She even called the office of the man she was scheduled to marry and left a harsh message with his Indian secretary that she thought he was an old disgusting man, and that he should marry women, not girls. The Indian secretary obviously thought better of giving such a message to his employer, for seas did not part and mountains failed to erupt. Determined, Sara called back and asked to speak to the man himself! He was not in his office. Sara was informed that he would be in Paris for a few weeks. Father, wearying of Sara's behaviour, had our telephones disconnected. Sara was confined to her room.

My sister's reality loomed ahead. The day of the wedding arrived. The weeks of fretful mourning had done nothing to diminish Sara's beauty. If anything, she appeared more beautiful, almost translucent, a heavenly creature not made for this world. Because of weight-loss, her dark eyes dominated her face and her features seemed chiselled. There was no end to Sara's eyes, and I could see into her soul through her enormous black pupils. I saw fear there.

Our older sisters, various female cousins and aunties arrived early on the morning of the wedding to prepare the bride for the groom. My unwanted presence escaped the attention of the women, for I sat like a stone in the corner of the large dressing-room that had been converted into a preparation room for the bride.

No less than fifteen women were attending to the various wedding details. The first ceremony, the *halawa*, was performed by our mother and her oldest aunty. All of Sara's body hair had to be removed, except her eyebrows and head hair. A special mixture of sugar, rosewater and lemon juice that would be spread over her body was now boiling over a low fire in the kitchen. When the sweet paste had dried on her body, it would be removed, and Sara's body hair would be ripped off with the sticky mixture. The aroma was sweet-smelling, but Sara's yelps of pain made me shudder in fear.

The henna was prepared for the final rinse through Sara's luxuriant curls; her hair would now shine with beautiful highlights. Her nails were painted bright red – the colour of blood, I reflected gloomily. The pale-pink lacy wedding-gown hung from the doorway. The requisite diamond necklace with matching bracelet and earrings were gathered in a pile on the dressing-table. Although sent over weeks ago as a gift from the groom, the jewels remained unnoticed and untouched by Sara.

When a Saudi bride is happy, the preparation room is filled with the sounds of laughter and eager anticipation. For Sara's wedding, the mood was sombre; her attendants might as well have been preparing her body for the grave. Everyone spoke in whispers. There was no response from Sara. I found her oddly subdued in view of her spirited reactions during the past few weeks. Later, I understood her trance-like state.

Father, concerned that Sara would humiliate the family name by voicing her objections, or even insulting the groom, had instructed one of the Pakistani palace doctors to inject her with powerful tranquillizers throughout the day. Later we discovered that the same doctor had given the groom the tranquillizers in the form of pills for Sara. The groom was told that Sara was highly nervous with excitement over the wedding, and the medicine was prescribed for a queasy stomach.

Since the groom had never met Sara, in the coming days he must have assumed that she was an unusually quiet and docile young woman. But then, again, many old men in my country marry young girls; I am sure they are accustomed to the terror of their young brides.

The beating of drums signalled the arrival of guests. At last the women were finished with Sara. The delicate dress was slipped over her head, the zipper was raised and the pink slippers were placed on her feet. My mother fastened the diamond necklace around her neck. I loudly announced that the necklace might as well be a noose. One of my aunties thumped me on my head, and another twisted my ear, but there was no sound from Sara. We all gazed at her in awed silence. We knew no bride could be more beautiful.

A huge tent had been erected in the backyard for the ceremony. The garden was inundated with flowers sent from Holland. With thousands of overhanging coloured lights, the grounds were spectacular. Taking in the splendour, I forgot for a few moments the grimness of the situation.

The tent was already overflowing with guests. Women from the royal family, literally weighed down by diamonds, rubies and emeralds, were sharing a social event with commoners – a rare occasion. Lower classes of Saudi women are allowed to view our weddings so long as they remain veiled and do not socialize with the royals. One of my friends told me that sometimes men veil and join these women so that they can view our forbidden faces. Supposedly all the male guests were being entertained at a major hotel in the city, enjoying the same socializing as these women guests: talking, dancing and eating.

At weddings in Saudi Arabia, men celebrate at one location and women at another. The only men allowed at the women's celebration are the groom, his father, the father of the bride, and a religious man to perform the short ceremony. In this case, the groom's father was deceased, so only our father would accompany the groom when the time arrived for him to claim his bride.

Suddenly the slaves and servants began to uncover the food. There was a rush towards the feast. The veiled ones were the first to assault the food; these poor women were cramming food under their veils and into their mouths. Other guests began to sample smoked salmon from Norway, Russian caviare, quail eggs and other gourmet delicacies. Four large tables swayed with the weight of the food: appetizers were on the left, main courses in the middle, desserts to the right, and off to the side were the liquid refreshments. No alcohol was visible, of course. But many of the royal women carried small jewelled flasks in their handbags. Now and then, giggling, they would retire to the washrooms for a small sip.

Belly dancers from Egypt moved to the centre of the tent. The crowd of women of all ages quietened and watched the dancers' movements with mixed interest. This was my favourite part of the wedding, but most of the women seemed uncomfortable with the erotic display. We Saudis take ourselves too seriously, and look on fun and laughter with suspicion. But I was startled when one of my older aunties leaped into the crowd and joined in the swaying of the belly dancers. She was amazingly skilled, but I heard the mumble of disapproval from several of my relatives.

Once again the sound of drums filled the air, and I knew it was time for Sara to appear. All the guests looked to the villa entrance in expectation. It was not long before the doors opened wide and Sara, accompanied by our mother on one side and an aunt on the other, was escorted to the dais.

Since I last saw my sister, a cloud-like pink veil had been draped over her face, held in place by a pink pearl tiara. The sheer veil served only to enhance her remarkable beauty. There was a low hum as the guests whispered their approval of her appropriately tortured demeanour. After all, a young virgin bride should look the part: frightened to the core of her being.

Dozens of female relatives followed behind, filling the air with the desert sounds of excitement and celebration: the high-pitched trill which the women produced by flicking their tongues on the roofs of their mouths. Other women joined in with shrill cries. Sara stumbled but was kept upright by our mother.

Soon my father and the groom made their appearance. I knew the groom was older than my father, but I was decidedly revolted by my first sight of him. He looked ancient to my young eyes, and I thought he most resembled a weasel. I cringed at the thought of him physically touching my shy and sensitive sister.

The groom wore a leering smirk as he lifted my sister's veil. She was too drugged to react, and stood motionless, facing her new master. The real marriage ceremony had been performed weeks prior to the wedding; no women had been present. Only men had participated in that ceremony, for it was the signing of dowry agreements and exchange of legal papers. Today the few words would be spoken that would complete the marriage rite.

The religious man looked at Father as he spoke the token words that Sara was now married to the groom in exchange for the agreed-upon dowry. Then he glanced at the groom who, in response, replied that he accepted Sara as his wife and that she, from this time forward, would be under his care and protection. None of the men looked at Sara at any time during the ceremony.

Reading passages from the Koran, the man of religion then blessed my sister's marriage. All at once, the women began to shriek and ululate. Sara was married. The men looked on, pleased and smiling.

As Sara stood motionless, the groom removed a small pouch from the pocket of his *thobe* (a full-length shirt-like garment worn by Saudi men) and tossed gold coins to the guests. I shivered as I watched him smugly accept their congratulations on his marriage to such a beautiful woman. He took my sister by the arm and hurriedly began to lead her away.

Sara's eyes locked on to mine as she passed my way; I knew someone should help her, but I felt certain no-one would. Quite suddenly I remembered Sara's words to Father: 'Victory breeds hatred, for the conquered are unhappy.' In my grieving mind, I found no consolation in the knowledge that the groom would never know happiness in such a bitterly unjust union. There could not be punishment enough for him.

Chapter Four

Divorce

Father forbade us from visiting Sara for the first three months of her marriage. She needed time to adjust to her new life and responsibilities, he said, and the sight of her family would serve only to inflame her desire to return to a useless life of dreams. Our vocal distress over her bondage drew nothing more than passionless nods. Sara, in Father's view, was doing what women are born to do: serve and pleasure the male and produce his children.

Sara had taken nothing from her room. Perhaps she understood that the presence of her books and other objects of delight would only make her present actuality more bleak. To me, it was as if Sara were dead; her absence left a black gaping hole in my life. I mourned her passing by spending long hours in her room with her possessions. I began to take an interest in Sara's hobbies and felt myself assuming parts of her personality. I read her diary, and her dreams felt as if they were my own; I wept with the fury of one who questions the wisdom of a God who allows evil to conquer the innocent.

My mother instructed that Sara's door be locked after she found me in Sara's bed, in her nightdress, reading her art books.

We did not have to suffer through Father's imposed three-month waiting period to see Sara. Five weeks after her wedding, she attempted suicide.

I was in the garden, talking with some of the animals in our newly constructed private zoo, when suddenly Omar tripped completely out of his sandals in his haste to enter the front gate. His skin, which was usually deep bronze, looked pasty white. He brushed off his *thobe* and beat the sand out of his sandals on the side of the wall. He told me to run and find my mother.

Mother had a certain sense about her children, and when she saw Omar she asked him what was wrong with Sara.

No Arab will tell a relative the truth when a family member is sick, dying or dead. We are people who simply cannot handle being the bearer of bad tidings. If a child dies, the unlucky person who receives the task of notifying the family will begin by saying the child is not feeling well. After questioning, the person will acknowledge that a trip to the doctor is necessary and then later admit that the child is in hospital. After intense pleas from the family members for additional information, the messenger will finally say the illness is serious and the family had best prepare for a journey to the bedside of the loved one. Later the person will painfully admit that the loved one's life is in grave danger. It might take a period of several hours to discover the exact degree of seriousness. But no-one will ever admit to the death of a loved one. The furthest an Arab will go in delivering bad news is to prepare the family for worse news from the doctor.

Omar told my mother that Sara had eaten some rotten meat and was now in a private clinic in Jeddah. Father was sending Mother on a private plane within the hour. Mother tightened her lips and turned in a rush to gather her *abaaya* (cloak) and veil.

I screamed and clung to Mother, so that she relented and allowed me to go – with the promise that I would not make a scene in the clinic if Sara were desperately ill. I promised and ran to Sara's room, pounding and kicking at the locked door until one of the servants found the key. I wanted to take Sara's favourite art book to her.

Omar drove us to Father's office since he had forgotten to collect our travel papers. In Saudi Arabia, a man must write a letter granting permission for the females in his family to travel. Without the papers, we might be stopped at the Customs office and prevented from boarding the plane. Father also sent our passports since, as he told Mother, it might be necessary for us to take Sara to London for treatment. Rotten meat? London? I knew what was rotten, and it was Father's story. I thought my sister must surely be dead.

We flew to Jeddah in a small private plane. The ride was smooth, but the atmosphere inside the cabin was clouded with tension. My mother said little and kept her eyes shut for most of the flight. Only a few years before, she had taken her first car ride. Now I saw her lips moving and I knew that double prayers were being spirited to God: Mother was praying first for Sara to be alive and second for the plane to take us safely to Sara.

The pilot and co-pilot were American, and I was immediately attracted to their open friendly manner. They asked me if I wanted to sit in the cockpit. Mother nodded a reluctant permission to my frenzied foot-stamping and arm-flapping. I had never sat in the cockpit before. Ali always sat in the cockpit.

At first I was frightened at the sight of the open sky, and the plane felt like a toy between us and the hard earth. I gave a small cry of alarm and backed away. John, the larger of the two Americans, gave me a reassuring smile, and patiently explained the functions of the various buttons and gadgets. To my surprise, I found myself leaning over his shoulder, completely at ease. For one of the few occasions in my young life, I felt calm and comfortable in the presence of men. Sadly, I was fearful of my father, and I detested Ali and my other half-brothers. It was a strange feeling, yet I felt intoxicated with the knowledge that men, whom I had been brought up to think of as gods, could be so ordinary and non-threatening. This was something new to think about.

When I looked out of the window of the plane, I understood what grips the heart of the eagle as it soars overhead, and I experienced a wonderful sense of freedom. My thoughts drifted to Sara and the shocking realization that birds and beasts were freer than my sister. I made a vow to myself that I would be the master of my life, no matter what actions I would have to take or pain I would have to endure.

I joined my mother for the landing of the plane; she gathered me into her loving arms and held me tenderly as the plane taxied to the terminal. She was veiled, but I knew her every expression, and I heard her breathe a long tortured sigh.

I said goodbye to the kindly Americans. I hoped they would fly us back to Riyadh, for I felt a camaraderie with the two men who had lent such importance to a child's foolish and feverish questions.

Arriving at the clinic, we heard wails and crying as we walked down the long corridor. Mother stepped up her pace and gripped my hand so tightly I wanted to complain.

Sara was alive, but barely. We were distraught to discover that she had tried to take her life by placing her head in the gas oven. She was very quiet, deathly pale. Her husband was not there, but he had sent over his mother. Now, in a loud voice, the old woman began to scold Sara harshly for embarrassing her son and his family. She was a mean old hag. I wanted to scratch her face and see her run, but I remembered my promise to Mother. Instead I stood, barely breathing from anger, patting Sara's smooth still hands.

Mother threw her veil over her head and faced the old woman. She had fretted over many possibilities, but the discovery that her daughter had attempted suicide was unexpected and devastating. When she turned in a cold fury to the husband's mother, I wanted to stamp and cheer. She stopped the woman cold when she asked what her son had done to make a young girl want to take her life. She ordered her to leave Sara's bedside, for this was no place for the ungodly. The old woman left without replacing her veil. We could hear her voice rise in anger as she cried out to God for sympathy.

Mother turned to me and saw my admiring smile. I was awed by her anger, and for a brief shining moment I felt God would not desert us. Sara would be saved. But I knew Mother's life would be one of misery when Father heard of her words. Knowing Father, he would be angry, not sympathetic, towards Sara for her desperate act, and he was sure to be furious with Mother for defending her daughter. In Saudi Arabia, the elderly are truly revered. No matter what they do or say, or how they behave, no-one dares confront someone of age. When she faced the old woman, my mother had been a tigress, protecting her young. My heart felt as though it would burst from pride at her courage.

After three days, without calling once, Sara's husband came to the clinic to claim his property. By the time he arrived, Mother had discovered the source of Sara's agony. She confronted her son-in-law with contempt. Sara's new husband was sadistic. He had subjected my sister to sickening sexual brutality until she felt her only escape was death. Even Father was repelled when he heard of his daughter's sufferings. But Father agreed with his son-in-law that a wife belonged with her husband. Sara's husband promised Father that his relations with her would conform to a life of normalcy.

Mother's hand trembled and her mouth stretched in a howl when Father told her of his decision. Sara began to weep and tried to leave the bed, saying she did not wish to live. She threatened to slit her wrists if forced to return to her husband. Mother stood over her daughter like a mountain and, for the first time in her life, defied her husband. She told him that Sara would never return to the house of a monster, and that she, Mother, would go to the king and the Council of Religious Men with the story, and neither would allow such a matter to continue. Father threatened Mother with divorce. She stood fast and told him to do whatever he had to do, but her daughter would not return to swim in such evil.

Father stood, unblinking. He probably realized that, in all likelihood, Sara would be forced by the men of religion to return to her husband. If the past were any precedent, they would advise the husband to deal with his wife in the manner spelled out by the Koran, and then they would turn their backs on such a disagreeable situation. Father stood, staring, analysing Mother's resolve. Askance at her apparent resoluteness, and wanting to avoid public interference in a family matter, for once in their married life he gave in.

Since we were of the royal family and he did not wish to sever his ties with my father, the husband reluctantly agreed to divorce Sara.

Islam gives the right of divorce to men, without any question of motive. Yet it is very difficult for a woman to divorce her husband. Had Sara been forced to file for the separation, many difficulties would have arisen, for the religious authorities might have ruled, 'You might dislike a thing which Allah has meant for your own good,' and forced Sara to remain with her husband. But Sara's husband relented and uttered the words 'I divorce you' three times in the presence of two male witnesses. The divorce was final in a matter of moments.

Sara was free! She returned to our home.

Every upheaval is a transition. My young world was transformed by Sara's wedding, attempted suicide, and divorce. Fresh thoughts and ideas began to grow in my mind; I was never to think as a child again.

For hours I pondered the primitive traditions surrounding marriage in my land. Numerous factors determine the marriageability of a girl in Saudi Arabia: her family name, her family fortune, her lack of deformities, and her beauty. Social dating is taboo, so a man must depend on his eagle-eyed mother and sisters constantly to seek out proper matches for him. Even after the promise to marry is made and the date is set, rarely does a girl meet her future husband prior to the wedding, though there are times when individual families allow the exchange of pictures.

If a girl is of a good family and without deformity, she will enjoy a number of marriage proposals. If she is a beauty, many men will send their mother or father to beg for marriage, for beauty is a great commodity for women in Saudi Arabia. Of course, no scandal can mar the reputation of the beauty or her desirability will fade; such a girl will find herself married as the third or fourth wife to an old man in a faraway village.

Many Saudi men leave the final decision on the marriage of their daughters to their wives, knowing they will make the best match possible for the family. Still, often the mother, too, will insist upon an unwanted marriage, even as her daughter protests. After all, she herself had married a man she feared, and her life had progressed without the anticipated horror or pain. Love and affection do not last, the mother will caution her daughter; it is best to marry into a family that they know. And then there are men, such as my father, who base their decision concerning their daughters' marriages upon possible personal or economic gain through the union, and there is no higher authority to question the verdict. Sara, for all her beauty, intelligence, and childhood dreams, in the end was no more than a pawn in my father's schemes for wealth.

This intimate view of my beloved sister's predicament filled me with a new resolve: it was my thought that we women should have a voice in the final decision on issues that would alter our lives for ever. From this time, I began to live, breathe and plot for the rights of women in my country so that we could live with the dignity and personal fulfilment that are the birthright of men.

Chapter Five

Ali

A few months after Sara's return, my oldest sister, Nura, convinced Father that Sara and I needed to see the world outside Saudi Arabia. None of us had been able to rouse Sara from her chronic depression, and Nura thought a trip would be just the right medicine. As to the extent of my travels, I had visited Spain twice, but I had been so young my recollections did not count.

Nura, married to one of our first king's grand-sons, pleased Father with her marriage and her calm placid outlook on life. She did as she was told, no questions asked. Father actually grew fond of her as the years passed, for few of his daughters had Nura's complaisant qualities. Since Sara's divorce, Father held Nura up as a constant reminder to the rest of his daughters. She had married a stranger, and her marriage had proved to be satisfactory. Of course, the real reason was that her husband was considerate and attentive.

In Father's mind, Sara had obviously provoked her husband into criminal behaviour. It is never the fault of the man in the Middle East. Even if he murders his wife, the man will state 'valid' reasons for his action, which will be accepted by other men without question. In my own country, I have seen newspapers print articles that honour a man for executing his wife or daughter for the crime of 'indecent behaviour'. The mere suspicion of sexual misconduct, such as kissing, can bring death to a young girl. In addition, public congratulations are given from the men of religion for the father's 'notable' act of upholding the commands of the Prophet!

Nura and Ahmed were in the midst of constructing a palace, and Nura wanted to travel to Europe to purchase Italian furnishings. On the way, we were to stop off in Egypt so that Nura's young children could view the pyramids.

Father, with twenty-two daughters from four wives, was often overheard muttering: 'Women are a man's curse.' It did not help his attitude that his younger daughters were in a kind of rebellion against the absolute rule of men. Our talk and actions were unprecedented and unappreciated. Knowing full well we would never reach the heights we desired, our talk alone was a victory of sorts, for no Saudi women had ever approached the topics we discussed with such great abandon.

Nura wanted Mother to go abroad with us, but Mother had been strangely quiet since Sara's return. It was as if her one great rebellion against Father's rule had drained her life's blood. But she encouraged the trip, for she wanted Sara to see Italy. She thought I was too young and should stay at home, but as usual a temper tantrum accomplished the result I wanted. Sara showed little interest, even in the possibility of seeing the artistic wonders of Italy, but I was out of control with happiness.

My joy was shattered by Ali's smug announcement that he was going with us. Father thought I needed a chaperon. In an instant, I lost my mind at the thought of Ali's treacherous presence ruining my vacation, and I was determined to insult him in the worst way. I grabbed his new *ghutra* (headdress) and *igaal* (black cord that rests on the top of the *ghutra*) and raced through the house to my bathroom. I had no notion of what I was going to do with them, but a Saudi man is highly offended if anyone even touches his headdress. I felt an urge to hurt Ali as quickly as possible.

When Ali followed, shouting that he would tell Father, I slammed the bathroom door on him. Since he was wearing sandals, Ali's big toe was broken, and his hand was bruised. From his shouts and moans, the servants thought I was killing him. No-one came to Ali's rescue, though.

I don't know what came over me – perhaps the sound of the big bully groaning and begging for sympathy – but I flushed his headdress down the toilet. The *igaal* would not flush, even as I frantically pushed it with the plunger. The sodden cord became stuck in the toilet! When Ali saw what I had done, he lunged for me. We were struggling on the floor when I got the better of him by pulling and twisting his broken toe. Mother, hearing Ali's screams of agony, intervened and saved him from my years of pent-up wrath.

I knew I was in big trouble. I rationalized that my situation could not be any worse, so when Mother and Omar took Ali to the clinic to get his broken toe bandaged I crept into his room and gathered up his secret hoard of 'treasures' that were forbidden by both our religion and our country.

These 'treasures' were the usual objects that all young boys collect the world over, but their possession is a serious offence under the law of religion in Arabia. Long before, I had located Ali's collection of *Playboy*, *Penthouse* and other similar magazines. Recently I had discovered a new collection of slides. Curious, I had taken them to my bedroom; perplexed, I viewed them on the slide projector. Naked men and women were doing all kinds of strange things; one group of pictures even showed animals with women. Ali had obviously lent them to other boys on occasion, for he had clearly printed his name on every forbidden article.

I was too innocent at the time to know exactly what it all meant, but I knew these 'treasures' were bad because he had always kept his secret cache stacked in the same old tattered box labelled 'School Notes'. I was very familiar with his belongings, having sorted through his stuff for years. I carefully removed every magazine along with the slides. I also found seven miniature bottles of alcohol that Ali had brought home after a weekend trip to Bahrain. I smiled at my plan as I shoved everything in a paper bag.

In Saudi Arabia, mosques are built in every neighbourhood, for the Government has placed top priority on providing a mosque within walking distance of every Muslim male. With prayers to be offered five times a day, it is more convenient to complete all the prayers if a man is a short distance from the mosque. Even though prayers can be given at any location so long as the person faces Makkah, it is thought that access to a mosque is preferable.

Living in one of the wealthiest districts, we were served by a huge mosque made of white opalescent marble. Since it was about two o'clock in the afternoon, I knew the noon prayers were over; it would be safe to carry out my plan without being seen. Even the men of religion nap in the hot climate of Arabia.

I opened the mosque door with dread, and peeped in carefully before entering. Not yet veiled, I thought perhaps my presence would invite little curiosity. I already had my story ready in the event I was caught. If questioned, I would say I was hunting my new kitten that had wandered on to the mosque grounds.

Surprisingly, the mosque was cool and inviting. I had never been inside the huge building, but I had followed my father and Ali to prayer many times. From the age of six, Ali had been encouraged to perform the five daily prayers. I felt my breath sharpen as I recalled the hurt I had felt as I watched my father hold Ali's hand and lead him proudly through the grand entrance of the mosque – always leaving me, a lowly female, at the side of the road to stare after them in sorrow and anger.

Women are forbidden entry into mosques in my country. Even though Prophet Muhammad did not forbid women to pray publicly in the mosques, he did state that it was best for them to pray in the privacy of their homes. As a result, no female in Saudi Arabia has ever been allowed inside a mosque.

No-one was around. I hurriedly walked across the marble floor; the clicking of my sandals sounded loud and strange. I placed the bag containing Ali's forbidden articles in the stairwell leading to the balcony that contains the loudspeakers which broadcast Prophet Muhammad's words throughout our cities five times a day. Just thinking of the intensity of the appeals of the muezzin, the criers who call the faithful to pray, I began to feel guilty about my adventure. Then I remembered Ali's superior smirk as he told me that Father would have me flogged and that he, Ali, would request the pleasure of beating me. I walked back home with a satisfied grin. Let Ali get out of this one.

That night, before Father came home from the office, three *mutawas* (religious men) arrived at our gate. I and three of our Filipino servants peered through one of the upstairs windows as we watched them shout at Omar and gesture wildly at the heavens and then towards some books and magazines which they obviously held in distaste. I wanted to laugh, but kept my face straight and serious.

All foreigners and most Saudis are frightened of the *mutawas* for they have much power, and they watch everyone for signs of weakness. Even members of the royal family try to avoid their attention.

Two weeks earlier, one of our Filipino maids had inflamed some *mutawas* by wearing a knee-length skirt in the *souq*. A group of religious men struck her with a stick and sprayed her uncovered legs with red paint. While the government of Saudi Arabia does not allow tourists to enter our country, there are many women who work as nurses, secretaries or domestic help in our major cities. Many of these women feel the wrath of those who speak God's word yet despise those of our sex. If a woman is so bold as to defy our traditions by exposing uncovered arms or legs, she runs the risk of being struck and sprayed with paint.

This maid had soaked her legs in paint remover, but they were still red and raw-looking. She was convinced that somehow the religious police had traced her to her residence and now they had come to take her to gaol. She ran to hide under my bed. I wanted to tell her the nature of their visit, but my secret had to be guarded – even from the Filipino servants.

Omar was absolutely pallid when he came into the villa screaming for Ali. I saw Ali scuffling down the hallway, gingerly walking with the top of his right foot high in the air while balancing on his heel. I followed and gathered with Mother and Ali in the sitting-room, where Omar was on the phone, calling Father at his office. The *mutawas* had left, entrusting Omar with samples of the incriminating contraband: one magazine, several slides and one miniature bottle of liquor. The rest they kept as evidence of Ali's guilt. I glanced at Ali and saw his face drain of blood when he saw his 'secret treasures' spread out in disarray on Omar's lap.

Catching sight of me, Omar asked me to leave the room, but I clung to my mother's skirts and she patted me on the head. Mother must have hated the way Omar bossed her children and she looked defiantly into his eyes. He decided to ignore me. He told Ali to sit down, that Father was on his way home and the *mutawas* had gone to get the police. Ali was going to be arrested, he announced with booming certainty.

The silence in the room was like the calm before a tempest. For a short moment I was terrified, and then Ali regained his composure and practically spat at Omar, declaring: 'They cannot arrest me; I am a prince. Those religious fanatics are nothing more than pesky mosquitoes at my ankles.' The sudden thought came to me that gaol might do Ali good.

The squealing of Father's brakes signalled his arrival. Rushing into the room barely controlling his anger, he picked up the forbidden articles one by one. When he saw the magazine, he looked hard at Ali. He threw the whisky aside with contempt, for all the princes have liquor in their homes. But when Father held the slide up to the lamp-light, he screamed for Mother and me to leave the room. We could hear him striking Ali with his hands.

All in all, it had been a bad day for Ali.

The *mutawas* must have thought better of calling the police to arrest one of the royal sons, for they returned in a few hours with little besides pious fury leading their way. But even Father had a difficult time with the *mutawas* in excusing the slides of women copulating with animals.

The year was 1968, and King Faisal was not as tolerant with the misdeeds of the young princes as had been his elder brother, Sa'ud. The *mutawas* felt they were in a position of power, for both they and Father knew that his uncle, the king, would be outraged if the contents of the slides became common knowledge. The fears of the *mutawas* were well known regarding the present course of modernization of our land. King Faisal constantly cautioned his brothers and cousins to control their children to avoid the wrath of the religious men upon the heads of the royal men who ruled. The king assured the religious elders that he was leading our country into needed modernization, not degenerate Westernization; the best, not the worst, of the West. The *mutawas* saw proof of the decadent West in the behaviour of the royals. Ali's slide collection did nothing to put their minds at ease about the whispered decadence of the royal family.

We heard the *mutawas* argue long into the night over an appropriate punishment for the son of a prince. Ali was lucky to be a member of the family of Al Sa'ud. The *mutawas* knew that, unless the king gave his approval, no royal prince would be charged in the country's court system. Rarely, if ever, did such an event occur. But if Ali had been a member of a common Saudi family or a member of the foreign community he would have been ordered to serve a long prison sentence.

Our family was all too familiar with the sad story of the brother of one of our Filipino drivers. Four years ago, the brother, who worked for an Italian construction firm in Riyadh, had been arrested for possessing a pornographic film. The poor man was now serving a seven-year prison sentence. Not only was he languishing in prison, but he was also ordered to endure ten lashes every Friday. Our driver, who visited his brother every Saturday, wept as he told Ali that every time he saw his poor brother the man was black from his neck to his toes from the lashings of the previous day. He feared his brother would not live out the coming year.

Unfortunately for Ali, his guilt was established without a doubt – his name was boldly printed on every forbidden item. In the end, a compromise of sorts was made: Father gave a huge sum of money to the mosque, and Ali had to be present for prayers five times each day to appease the men of God, along with God himself. The *mutawas* knew that few of the younger royal princes bothered to go to prayer at all, and that such a punishment would be especially irksome to Ali. He was told he would have to show his face to the head *mutawa* in our mosque at every prayer for the next twelve months. His only excuse would be if he were out of the city. Since Ali generally slept until nine o'clock, he frowned at the mere thought of the sunrise prayer. In addition, he had to write one thousand times on a legal pad: 'God is great, and I have displeased Him by running after the corrupt and immoral ways of the Godless West.' As a final condition, Ali was told he would have to reveal the name of the person who had supplied him with the slides and magazines. As it was, Ali had slipped in the magazines from trips abroad since a prince is ushered through Customs with only a courtesy glance. But a Westerner he had befriended at a party had sold him the slides, and Ali, eager for a foreign villain to take the pressure off him, happily supplied the *mutawas* with the Westerner's name and work address. We would later learn that the man had been arrested, flogged and deported.

I felt terrible. My stupid prank had disgraced my entire family with a stinging humiliation. I did not think the lesson would harm Ali, but I knew my parents had been affected and other innocent people would be injured. Also, I am ashamed to admit, I was petrified that my guilt would be discovered. I prayed to God that, if He would let me escape capture this once, from that day forward I would be a perfect child.

Omar led the *mutawas* out of our grounds. Mother and I waited for Father and Ali to return to the family sitting-room. Father was breathing loudly and gripped Ali by his upper arm, pushing him towards the stairway. Ali looked my way, and our eyes met. A moment, a flash of

realization, and I understood that he had concluded I was the guilty party. Sadly, I saw that
he looked more hurt than angry.

I began to sob, for I felt the weight of the terrible
deed I had committed. Father looked at me in pity.
Then he shoved Ali and screamed that he had upset
the entire family, including the innocent children.
For the first time in my life, my father came and
held me in his arms and told me not to worry.

I was now truly miserable. The touch that I had
been longing for all my life now felt barren, and
the joy I had so often imagined was destroyed in
the elusive prize so wrongly taken.

My misdeed had accomplished my target, however. No mention was ever made of Ali's broken
toe or the toilet clogged with Ali's headdress. One
sin had so outweighed the other that they ended
up cancelling each other out.

Chapter Six

The Trip

Despite the recent family turmoil, the trip to Italy and Egypt was still planned, but my heart was no longer joyful. I organized my case and made my lists as I watched Ali warily trudge by my bedroom door. In the past, Ali had given me little thought. I was scorned as a girl, someone to antagonize or push about occasionally – a person of little worth. He looked at me differently now, for he had made the surprising discovery that I, a lowly female and the youngest member of the family, was a dangerous and worthy opponent.

On the day of our departure, six limousines were needed to transport us to the airport. Eleven of us were travelling for four weeks: Nura and Ahmed, with three of their five children; two of their Filipino maids; Sara and myself; and Ali and his friend Hadi.

Two years older than Ali, Hadi was a student at the Religious Institute, a boys' school in Riyadh for those young men who aspired to become *mutawas*. Hadi impressed adults by quoting the Koran and acting very piously in their presence. My father felt confident that Hadi would have a good influence on his children. To those who would listen, Hadi loudly expressed his viewpoint that all women should be confined to the home; he told Ali that women were the cause of all evil on earth.

I could tell it was going to be a pleasant and enjoyable trip with both Ali and Hadi around.

Mother did not accompany us to the airport. For the past few days, she had been listless and sad; I assumed Ali's antics had worried her. She said her farewells in the garden and waved us off from the front gate. She was veiled, but I knew tears were falling on her face. Something was amiss with Mother, I felt, but I had no time to dwell on the possibilities as the prospect of this exciting trip lay ahead of us.

Ahmed had recently purchased a new plane, so our flight was strictly a family affair. I looked to see if the two Americans who had flown Mother and me to Jeddah were piloting; disappointed, I saw they were not. Two British pilots were in the cockpit and they looked friendly enough. The royal family hired a large number of American and British citizens as private pilots. Ahmed conferred with the two men while Nura and the maids settled in with her three little ones.

Sara, her veil now removed, was already bundled in a blanket, clutching her precious books. Hadi looked with distaste at her uncovered face and whispered angrily to Ali, who in turn ordered Sara to replace her veil until we left Saudi Arabia. Sara told Ali she could not see to read through the thick fabric, and if he were smart he would shut his ugly mouth.

Even before we had left the ground there was already a family squabble. I tried to stamp on Ali's sore toe but missed, and Ali took a swipe at my head; I ducked, and he missed. Ahmed, as the oldest male authority figure, shouted at everybody to sit down and be quiet. He and Nura exchanged a look that let me know they were already rethinking the wisdom of their generous invitation.

The three holiest spots in Islam are Makkah, Madinah and Jerusalem. Makkah is the city that captures the hearts of more than a billion Muslims scattered over the globe, for it was there that God revealed His will to His Prophet, Muhammad. The foundations of our religious life are five ritual obligations, called the pillars of religion. One of these obligations requires that every Muslim with the financial ability must attend Haj. No good Muslim feels complete without making the pilgrimage to Makkah at least once in his lifetime.

Our second-holiest city, Madinah, considered 'the city of the Prophet', is the place of Muhammad's burial.

And Jerusalem is our third-holiest city. It was in Jerusalem that Muhammad was taken up by God to heaven on the Dome of the Rock. Muslims weep bitter tears at the mention of Jerusalem, for it is a city now occupied and no longer free and open to our people.

If Makkah, Madinah and Jerusalem are a Muslim's spiritual fountainheads, then Cairo is the crowning glory of a Muslim's self-esteem. Cairo represents fifty centuries of titanic duration, and presents Arabs with the marvel of one of the greatest civilizations to appear on the earth. Egypt is a source of great pride for all Arabs. The might, wealth and accomplishments of the ancient Egyptians make the oil wealth of the modern Gulf Arabs seem puny and inconsequential.

It was in Cairo, that city bursting with life from the beginning of time, that I became a woman. In the Arab culture, with so much importance attached to the change from girlhood to womanhood, every young girl awaits with a combination of dread and deep satisfaction the sight of her first blood. When my Western women friends tell me that they did not know what was happening to them when their first blood appeared, and that they were convinced they were dying, I am struck dumb with surprise. The coming of women's menses is a source of easy conversation in the Muslim world. Suddenly, at that moment, a child is transformed into an adult. There is no going back to that warm cocoon of childhood innocence.

In Saudi Arabia, the appearance of the first menses means that it is time to select the first veil and *abaaya* – with the greatest of care. Even the shopkeepers, Muslim men from India or Pakistan, enquire with ease and respect as to the time the girl-child became a woman. In all seriousness, the shopkeeper will smile indulgently, and proceed to select the *abaaya* and veil that will show the child to her greatest advantage.

Even though the only colour for a veil is black,

there are many possibilities for fabric selection and weight of material. The veil can be of thin material, giving the world a shadowy glimpse of the forbidden face. A medium-weight fabric is more practical, for one can see through the gauzy cloth without the rude glances or sharp remarks from the keepers of the faith. If a woman chooses the traditional thick black fabric, no man can imagine her features under a facial mask that refuses to move with the strongest of breezes. Of course, this selection makes it impossible to examine jewellery in the gold *souq* or to see speeding cars after dusk. In addition to this traditional heavy veil, some of the conservative women choose to wear black gloves and thick black stockings so that no hint of flesh is visible to the world.

For women with a need to express their individuality and fashion sense, there are ways to avoid that endless sea of conformity in dress through creative design. Many purchase scarves with jewelled decorations, and the movement of trinkets turns the heads of most men. Expensive eye-catching decorations are often sewn to the sides and back of the *abaaya*.

Younger women, in particular, strive to set themselves apart by their unique selections. The male shopkeeper will model the latest designer fashions in veils and *abaaya* and show the young girl the stylish way of throwing the scarf over her head to project a look of smart fashion. The method of tying the *abaaya* to show the exact amount of foot that is allowed without being considered risqué is discussed in great detail. Every young girl experiments to find her own method of wearing the *abaaya* with flair.

A child enters the shop, but a woman emerges, veiled and, on that day, of a marriageable age. Her life changes in that split second. Arab men barely glance at the child as she enters the shop but once she dons her veil and *abaaya* discreet glances come her way. Men now attempt to catch a glimpse of a forbidden, suddenly erotic ankle. With the veil, we Arab women become overwhelmingly tantalizing and desirable to Arab men.

But I was now in Cairo, not home in Saudi Arabia, so the full impact of my first blood did little more than irritate me. Sara and Nura showed me all the things a woman should do. They both warned me against telling Ali, as if I would, for they knew he would try to make me veil immediately, even in Cairo. Sara looked at me with great sadness and gave me a long hug. She knew that from that day forward I would be considered a threat and danger to all men until I was safely wed and cloistered behind walls.

In Cairo, Ahmed owned a luxurious apartment that spread over three floors inside the city centre. For privacy, Ahmed and Nura settled on the top floor. The two Filipino maids, Nura's three babies, Sara and I occupied the second floor. Ali, Hadi and the Egyptian caretaker stayed on the first floor. Sara and I hugged each other with delight when we realized Ali and Hadi were separated from us by an entire floor.

On our first evening, plans were made for Ahmed, Nura, Hadi and Ali to go to a night-club to watch belly dancing. Ahmed thought that Sara and I should stay at home with the babies and the Filipino servants. Sara made no protest, but I pleaded our case so eloquently that Ahmed relented.

At fourteen, I came alive in the land of the pharaohs and joyfully anointed Cairo as my favourite city of all time. That attachment to Cairo has never wavered. The excitement of this city inflamed me with a passion I had never known before, and which I cannot fully explain to this day. Men and women of every colour and dress roamed the streets, searching for adventure and opportunity. I recognized that my life before had been dry, without stimulation, for I saw that Cairo was the opposite of our Arabian cities, which were, to my young eyes, sterile and lifeless.

I found the grinding poverty unsettling, yet it was not discouraging, for I saw in it a profound force of life. Poverty can turn a person into a flaming torch for change and revolution, without which mankind would come to a standstill. I thought again of Saudi Arabia and knew that some degree of poverty or need should seep into our lives and force us to renew our spiritual life.

Yes, there are many classes of people in my land, from those various levels of the wealthy royal family down to that of lowly salaried workers. But no-one, including foreign workers, is without the basic necessities of life. Our government ensures the wellbeing of all Saudis. Each male citizen is assured of a home, health care, education, a business where he can earn a living, interest-free loans and even money for food, should the need arise. Our female citizens are provided for by the men of their family, whether it be father, husband, brother or cousin.

As a result of this satisfaction of basic needs, the spark of life generated by material desire is hopelessly lacking in my land. Because of this, I despaired that the pages of history would ever turn on my land. We Saudis are too rich, too settled in our apathy for change. As we drove through the bustling city of Cairo, I mentioned this idea to my family, but I saw that only Sara listened and understood the essence of my thoughts.

The sun was now setting, and the sky turned to gold behind the sharp outline of the pyramids. The generous slow-moving Nile was breathing life throughout the city and into the desert. Watching it, I felt life rush through my veins.

Ali and Hadi were furious that Sara and I – two unmarried females – had been allowed to go into the nightclub. Hadi spoke long and seriously to Ali about the deterioration of our family's values. He declared with smug satisfaction that his sisters had all been married by the age of fourteen, and that they were guarded carefully by the men of his family. He said that, as a man of religion, he had to protest to our father when we returned from the trip. Sara and I, bold in our distance from Riyadh, made faces and told him he had not yet become a religious man. We told him, in slang we had learned from watching American movies, 'to save it'.

Hadi devoured the dancers with his eyes, and made crude remarks about their body parts, yet he swore to Ali that they were nothing but whores, and that if he had his way they would be stoned. Hadi was a pompous ass. Even Ali tired of his holier-than-thou attitude and began to thump his fingers on the table with impatience and to look around the room.

After Hadi's comments and attitude, I was staggered by his actions the following day.

Ahmed hired a chauffeur-driven limousine to take Nura, Sara and me shopping. Ahmed went to meet a businessman. The caretaker, who doubled as a driver, took the two Filipinos and the three children to the pool at the Mena House Hotel. When we left the apartment, Ali and Hadi were lounging about, exhausted from the previous late night.

The sweltering heat of the city soon tired Sara, and I offered to go back to the apartment and keep her company until Nura finished her shopping. Nura agreed, and sent the driver to drop us off. He would return to collect Nura afterwards.

When we entered the apartment, we heard muffled screams. Sara and I followed the noise to Hadi and Ali's room. The door was unlocked, and we suddenly realized what was happening before our eyes. Hadi was raping a young girl, no more than eight years old, and Ali was holding her.

Blood was everywhere. Our brother and Hadi were laughing.

At the sight of this traumatic scene, Sara became hysterical and began to scream and run. Ali's face became a mask of fury as he shoved me from the room, knocking me to the floor. I ran after Sara. We huddled in our room.

When I could no longer endure the sounds of terror that continued to filter up to our floor, I crept back down the stairwell. I was desperately trying to think of a course of action when the doorbell rang. I saw Ali answer the door to an Egyptian woman, about forty years of age. He handed the woman fifteen Egyptian pounds and asked her if she had more daughters. She said that she did and that she would return tomorrow. Hadi ushered out the weeping child. The mother, showing no emotion, took the child, who was limping, tears streaming down her face, by the hand and closed the door behind her.

Ahmed did not seem surprised when Nura, angry, told him the story. He pursed his lips and said he would find out the details. Later he told Nura that the mother herself had sold her child and that there was nothing he could do.

Even though caught in this shameful act, Hadi and Ali acted as though nothing had happened. When I sneered at Hadi and asked him how he could be a religious man, he laughed full in my face. I turned to Ali and told him that I was going to tell Father he was attacking young girls, and he laughed even harder than Hadi. He leaned towards me and said: 'Tell him! I do not mind!' He said that Father had given him the name of a man to contact for the same type of service. He smiled and said young girls were more fun and, besides, Father always did the same sort of thing when he came to Cairo.

I felt as though I had been electrocuted; my brain felt burned, my mouth hung open, and I stared blankly at my brother. I had my first thoughts that all – *all* – men are wicked. I wanted to destroy my memory of that day and lapse once again into the innocence of the mists of my childhood. I walked softly away. I came to dread what I might discover next in the cruel world of men.

I still cherished Cairo as a city of enlightenment, but the decay brought by poverty caused me to rethink my earlier notions. Later in the week, I saw the Egyptian mother knocking on doors in the building with another young girl in tow. I wanted to question her, to discover how a mother could sell her young. She saw my determined look of enquiry and hurried away.

Sara and I talked with Nura for long hours about the phenomenon, and Nura sighed and said that Ahmed told her it was a way of life in much of the world. When I shouted indignantly that I would rather starve than sell my young, Nura agreed, but said it was easy to say such things when the pangs of hunger were not in your stomach.

We left Cairo and its woes behind us. Sara finally had the opportunity to realize her visions of Italy. Was her radiant look worth the travail that had freed her to come here? She dreamily proclaimed that the reality soared above her fantasies.

We toured the cities of Venice, Florence and Rome. The gaiety and the laughter of the Italians still ring in my ears. I think their love of life one of the earth's great blessings, far overshadowing their contributions to art and architecture. Born in a land of gloom, I am consoled by the idea of a nation that does not take itself too seriously.

In Milan, Nura spent more money in a matter of days than most people earn in a lifetime. It was as if she and Ahmed shopped in a frenzy, with a deep desire to fill some lonely void in their lives.

Hadi and Ali spent their time buying women, for the streets of Italy were filled, by day or by night, with beautiful young women available to those who could pay. I saw Ali as I always had, a selfish young man, concerned only with his pleasure. But Hadi, I knew, was far more evil, for he bought the women yet condemned them for their role in the act. He desired them, yet hated them and the system that left them free to do as they would. His hypocrisy was to me the essence of the evil nature of men.

When our plane touched down in Riyadh, I prepared myself for more unpleasantness. At fourteen, I knew that I would now be considered a woman, and that a hard fate awaited me. As precarious as my childhood had been, I had a sudden longing to cling to my youth and not let go. I had no doubt that my life as a woman would be a perpetual struggle against the social order of my land, which sacrifices those of my sex.

My fears regarding my future soon paled with the agony of the moment. I arrived home to discover that my mother was dying.

Chapter Seven

Journey's End

Our one certainty in life is death. As a staunch believer in the words of the Prophet Muhammad, my mother felt no apprehension at the end of her life's journey. She had followed the pure life of a good Muslim and knew her just reward awaited her. Her sorrow was intertwined with her fears for her unmarried daughters. She was our strength, our only support, and she knew that we would be tossed in the wind at her passing.

Mother confessed that she had felt her life ebbing even as we departed on our travels. She had no basis for her knowledge, other than three very extraordinary visions that came to her as dreams.

Mother's parents had died of fever when she was eight years of age. As the only female child, Mother had nursed her parents during their brief illness. They both seemed to be recovering when, in the middle of a swirling fury of a blinding sandstorm, her father had risen on his elbows, smiled at the heavens, uttered four words – 'I see the garden' – and died. Her mother died shortly afterwards without revealing a hint of what she witnessed awaiting her. My mother, left in the care of her four older brothers, was married at an early age to my father.

Mother's father had been a compassionate and kind man. He had loved his daughter as he did his sons. When other men of the tribe sulked at the birth of their daughters, Grandfather laughed and told them to praise God for the blessing of a tender touch in their home. Mother said she would never have been married at such an early age had her father lived. He would have given her some years of the freedom of childhood for herself, she believed.

Sara and I were sitting by her bedside as Mother haltingly confided her disturbing dreams. The first of her visions came four nights before we received word of Sara's attempted suicide.

'I was in a bedouin tent. It was the same as our family tent of my childhood. I was surprised to see my father and mother, young and healthy, sitting beside the coffee fire. I heard my brothers in the distance, bringing in the sheep from a day of grazing. I made a rush for my parents, but they could not see me, nor could they hear me as I cried out their names.

'Two of my brothers, the ones now deceased, came into the tent and sat with my parents. My brothers sipped warm milk from the she-camel, in small cups, while my father pounded the beans for the coffee. The dream ended as Father quoted a verse he had made up about the Paradise awaiting all good Muslims. The verse was simple, yet reassuring to my mind. It went:

Pleasant rivers flow,
Trees shade the yellow of the sun.
Fruit gathers around the feet,
Milk and honey knows no end.
Loved ones are waiting, for those trapped
on earth.'

The dream ended. Mother said she thought little
of it, other than that it might be a message of joy
from God to assure her that her parents and family
were in Paradise.

About a week after Sara came home, Mother
experienced a second vision. This time, all the
members of her deceased family were sitting in
the shade of a palm tree. They were eating wonderful food from silver dishes. But this time they
saw her, and Mother's father got to his feet and
came to greet her. He took her by the hand and
tried to get her to sit and to eat.

Mother said she became frightened in the dream
and tried to run away, but her father's hand tightened. Mother remembered that she had young to
care for and begged her father to release her, told
him that she had no time to sit and eat. She said her
mother stood and touched her shoulder and told
her: 'Fadeela, God will care for your daughters.
The moment is coming for you to leave them in
His care.'

Mother awoke from her dream. She said she
knew at that instant that her time on earth was
passing and that she would soon go to those who
went before her.

Two weeks after we left on our trip, Mother began to experience back and neck pains. She felt dizzy and sick. The pain was her message; she knew her time was short. She went to the doctor and told him of her dreams and the new pain. He dismissed the dreams with a wave of his hand, but became serious at the description of the pain. Special tests soon revealed that Mother had an inoperable tumour on her spine.

Mother's most recent dream came the night the doctor confirmed her terminal illness. In the dream, she was sitting with her heavenly family, eating and drinking with great gaiety and abandon. She was in the company of her parents, grand-parents, brothers and cousins – relatives who had died many years before. Mother smiled as she saw little ones crawling along the ground and chasing butterflies in a meadow. Her mother smiled at her and said: 'Fadeela, why do you not pay attention to your babies? Do you not recognize those of your very blood?'

Mother suddenly realized that the children were indeed hers – they were the ones lost to her in their infancy. They gathered in her lap, those heavenly five babies, and she began to sway and swing and hold them close.

Mother was going to the ones lost and losing the ones she had known. She was leaving us.

Mercifully, Mother suffered little at her death. I like to think that God saw she had passed the harsh trials of life as a person of godliness and felt no need to wound her further with the pain of passing.

Her daughters surrounded every inch of the deathbed – she lay cloaked with the love of her own flesh and blood. Her eyes lingered on each of us, no words were spoken, but we felt her farewells. When her gaze rested upon my face, I saw her worries gather as a storm, for she knew that I, unbending to the wind, would find life harder than most.

Mother's body was washed and prepared for her return to earth by the older aunties of our family. I saw her as they wrapped the white linen shroud around her thin body, worn down by childbearing and disease. Her face was peaceful, now free of earthly worries. I thought Mother appeared younger in death than in life. It was difficult for me to believe that she had given birth to sixteen children, of whom eleven had survived.

Our immediate family, along with all of Father's wives and their children, gathered in our home; a verse from the Koran was read to offer comfort. Mother's shroud-wrapped body was then placed in the back seat of a black limousine and driven away by Omar.

Our custom forbids females at the burial-site, but my sisters and I showed an unyielding front to our father; he relented on the promise that we would not wail or pull out our hair. And so it was that our entire family followed the car of death, a sad but silent caravan, into the desert.

In Islam, to show grief at a loved one's passing indicates displeasure with the will of God. Besides, our family comes from the Najd region of Saudi Arabia, and our people do not publicly mourn the passing of loved ones.

A freshly dug grave in the endless desert of our land had already been prepared by the Sudanese servants. The body of our mother was tenderly lowered, and the white cloth covering her face was removed by Ali, her only earthly son. My sisters huddled far from Mother's final resting-place, but my eyes could not leave the grave-site. I was the last child born of her body; I would stay with her earthly cloak until the final moment. I flinched as I watched the slaves push the red sands of the Empty Quarter over her face and body.

As I watched the sands cover the body of one I so adored, I suddenly remembered a beautiful verse by the great Lebanese philosopher Kahlil Gibran: 'Mayhap a funeral among men is a wedding feast among the angels.' I imagined my mother at the side of her mother and father, with her own little ones gathered in her arms. Certain at that moment that I would, another day, feel the loving touch of Mother, I ceased weeping and walked towards my sisters, shocking them with my smile of joy and serenity. I quoted the powerful verse God had sent to erase my pain, and my sisters nodded in perfect understanding at the wise Kahlil Gibran's words.

We were leaving Mother behind in the empty vastness of the desert, yet I knew it no longer mattered that there was no stone placed to mark her presence there, or that no religious services were held to speak of the simple woman who had been a flame of love during her time on earth.

Her reward was that she was now with her other loved ones, waiting there for us.

Ali seemed at a loss for once, and I knew his pain was keen also. Father had little to say and avoided our villa from the day of Mother's death. He sent us messages through his second wife, who had now replaced Mother as the head of his wives.

Within the month, we learned through Ali that Father was preparing to wed again, for four wives are common with the very wealthy and the very poor bedouin in my land. The Koran says that each wife must be treated as the others. The affluent of Saudi Arabia have no difficulty in providing equality for their wives. The poorest bedouin have only to erect four tents and provide simple fare. For these reasons, you find many of the richest and the poorest Muslims with four wives. It is only the middle-class Saudi who has to find contentment with one woman, for it is impossible for him to find the funds to provide middle-class standards for four separate families.

Father was planning to marry one of the royal cousins, Randa, a girl with whom I had played childhood games in what seemed like another lifetime. Father's new bride was fifteen, only one year older than I, his youngest child of my mother.

Four months after the burial of my mother, I attended the wedding of my father. I was surly and refused to join in the festivities – I was awash with pent-up emotions of animosity. After the birth of sixteen children and many years of obedient servitude, I knew that the memory of my mother had been effortlessly disregarded by my father.

Not only was I furious at my father; I also felt overwhelming hatred towards my former playmate Randa, who was now going to be the fourth wife, filling the void created by my mother's death.

The wedding was grand, the bride was young and beautiful. My anger towards Randa collapsed as my father led her from the huge ballroom to the marriage bed. My eyes widened as they saw her worried face. Her lips trembled with fear! As a roaring flame is instantaneously extinguished, the sight of Randa's obvious despair quietened and transformed my passion from black hate to tender commiseration. I felt ashamed of my hostility, for I saw that she was as the rest of us, helpless in the face of towering, dominating Saudi manhood.

Father travelled with his virginal bride on an extended honeymoon to Paris and Monte Carlo. In my propitious change of emotion, I waited for Randa's return, and as I lingered I vowed to awaken Father's new wife to a path of purpose: freedom for women in our land. Not only would I provide Randa with new challenges and dreams of power; I also knew I would wound Father in the political and spiritual awakening of his young wife. I could not forgive him for so easily forgetting the wonderful woman who was my mother.

Chapter Eight

Girlfriends

Upon their return from their honeymoon, Father and Randa moved into our villa. Even though Mother was no longer with the living, her younger children continued to reside in Father's villa, and his new wife was expected to assume the duties of a mother. Since I was the youngest child, only one year behind Randa, the custom seemed ludicrous in our situation. However, there is no room for manoeuvring or change to fit the individual conditions in Saudi Arabia, so Randa was installed in our home, a child masquerading as a woman and mistress of our large household.

Randa returned from her honeymoon quiet, almost broken. She rarely talked, never smiled, and moved slowly through the villa, as though she might cause some injury or harm. Father seemed pleased with his new possession, for he spent many hours cloistered in his living-quarters with his youthful bride.

After the third week of Father's undivided attention to Randa, Ali cracked a joke about Father's sexual prowess. I asked my brother what he thought of Randa's feelings in the matter – to be wed to one so much older, one she did not know or love.

Ali's vacant expression told me all too clearly not only that the thought had never entered his head, but also that such a consideration would not find fertile ground in his narrow realm of understanding. He well reminded me that nothing would ever penetrate that dark sea of egotistical matter that constitutes the mind of a Saudi man.

Randa and I held different philosophies. She believed: 'What is written on your forehead, your eyes will see.' I think: 'The picture in your mind will be photographed by your life.' In addition, Randa was painfully shy and timid, whereas I greet life with a certain fierceness.

I noticed Randa's eyes as they followed the hands of the clock; she began to fidget a few hours prior to Father's usual arrival-times for lunch and for the evening meal. She had orders from my father to eat her meals before his arrival and then to shower and prepare herself for him.

At noon each day Randa would order the cook to serve her lunch. She would eat sparingly and then retire to her quarters. My father generally arrived at the villa around one o'clock, had his lunch, and then went to his new wife. He would leave the villa around five o'clock and return to his offices. (In Saudi Arabia, the workdays are divided into two shifts: from 9 a.m. until 1 p.m. and, after a four-hour afternoon break, from 5 p.m. until 8 p.m.)

Observing Randa's pinched look, I thought of asking Father about the teachings of the Koran – the instructions from God that each Muslim was supposed to divide his days and evenings among four wives. Since the day he had wed Randa, his three older wives had been virtually ignored. After consideration, I thought better of my boldness.

And so the evenings were a repeat of the lunch-break. Randa would call for her dinner around eight o'clock, eat, and go to her rooms for her bath and preparation for her husband. I generally would not see her again until after my father left for work the next morning. She had orders to wait in the bedroom until he had left.

The anxiety of watching Randa's bleak life unfold spurred me on to mischief. I had two girlfriends who frightened even me with their boldness; their liveliness might encourage Randa to become more assertive. Little did I know what forces I would unleash by forming a girls' club with Randa, my two indomitable friends and myself as the sole members.

We called our club 'Lively Lips', for we had as our goal to talk ourselves into bravery to battle the silent acceptance of the role of women in our society. We solemnly vowed to uphold the following goals:

(1) At every opportunity, let the spirit of women's rights move our lips and guide our tongues.

(2) Each member should strive to bring in one new member per month.

(3) Our first goal would be to stop marriages of young women to old men.

We young women of Arabia recognized that the men of our land would never pursue social change for our sex, that we would have to force change. As long as Saudi women accepted their authority, men would rule. We surmised that it was the responsibility of each individual woman to foment desire for control of her life and other female lives within her small circle. Our women are so beaten down by centuries of mistreatment that our movement had to begin with an awakening of the spirit.

My two friends, Nadia and Wafa, were not of the royal family, but were children of prominent families in the city of Riyadh.

Nadia's father owned a huge contracting company. Because of his willingness to give large kickbacks to various princes, his company was awarded large government building contracts. He employed thousands of foreign workers from Sri Lanka, the Philippines and Yemen. Nadia's father was almost as wealthy as the royals; he easily supported three wives and fourteen children. Nadia was seventeen, the middle of seven daughters. She had watched with dismay as her three older sisters were married off for the purposes of family connections and convenience. Surprisingly, all three marriages had suited her sisters and they were happy, with good husbands. Nadia said that kind of luck would never continue. She felt with increasing pessimism that she would end up with an old, ugly and cruel husband.

Nadia was indeed more fortunate than most Saudi women; her father had determined that she could continue her education. He had told her she did not have to marry until she was twenty-one. This imposed deadline stirred Nadia into action.

She declared that, since she had only four more years of freedom left, she was going to taste every aspect of life during that time to provide dreams for the remainder of a dull life married to an old man.

Wafa's father was a leading *mutawa*, and his extremism had driven his daughter to extremes of her own. Her father had only one wife, Wafa's mother, but he was a cruel and vicious man. Wafa swore she wanted nothing to do with a religion that appointed such men as her father as a leader. Wafa believed in God and thought Muhammad had been His messenger, but she thought that somehow Muhammad's messages had been conveyed incorrectly by his followers, for no God would wish such grief on women, half of the world's people.

Wafa needed to look no farther than her own home. Her mother was never allowed out of the house; she was a virtual prisoner, enslaved by a man of God. There were six children, five of whom were adult sons. Wafa had been a late surprise to her parents, and her father was so disappointed that he had a girl-child he had virtually ignored her except to give her orders. She was ordered to stay in the home and learn to sew and cook. From the age of seven, Wafa was forced to wear an *abaaya* and to cover her hair. Each morning from the time she was nine, her father would ask her if she had seen her first blood. He was alarmed that his daughter would venture out, face uncovered, after she was classified by God as a woman.

Wafa was allowed few friends. What rare friends she had soon drifted away since Wafa's father made a habit of boldly enquiring in her friends' presence about their first blood.

Wafa's mother, weary and exhausted from the rigid rules of her husband, had made a decision late in life silently to defy his demands. She assisted her daughter in sneaking out of the home and told her husband the child was sleeping or studying the Koran when enquiries concerning Wafa's whereabouts were voiced.

I imagined myself bold and rebellious, but Wafa and Nadia made my stance for women seem puny and powerless. They said that all I did was to provide intelligent stimulation – that my answer to a problem was to talk it to death – but that in reality my efforts to help women were useless. After all, my life had not changed. I realized they were right.

I will never forget one incident that occurred in an underground carpark close to the *souq* area, not far from the spot that foreigners call 'Chop Chop Square' since that is where our criminals lose their heads or their hands on Fridays, our day of religion.

I had hidden the passing of my first blood from my father, since I was in no rush to swathe myself in the black garb of our women. Unfortunately, Nura and Ahmed decided that I had postponed the inevitable long enough. Nura told me that if I did not tell my father immediately, she would. So I gathered my friends around me, including

Randa, and we made the mission to purchase my new 'life's uniform', black scarf on black veil on black *abaaya*.

Omar drove us to the entrance of the *souq* area, and we four young women disembarked, agreeing to meet him in two hours at the same spot. Omar always accompanied us into the *souq* to keep special watch on the women of the family, but that day he had an important errand to run and took the opportunity while we were shopping. Besides, Father's new wife was accompanying his daughter, and Omar was reassured by Randa's acquiescent presence. He had seen no indication that Randa was slowly awaking after the long dull sleep of submission.

We milled about the shops, hands examining the various scarves, veils and *abaayas*. I wanted something special, a way of being an original in the ocean of black-garbed women. I cursed myself for not having an *abaaya* made in Italy, from the finest Italian silk, with an artist's intricate designs, so that, when I breezed past, people would know there was an individual under the black covering, a woman with style and class.

Everyone was veiled except me, and as we made our way to the heart of the *souq* to continue our search I noticed that Wafa and Nadia, heads together, were whispering and giggling. Randa and I stepped up our pace, and I asked them what was so amusing. Nadia looked towards me and spoke through her veil. She said they were remembering a man they had met on their last trip to the *souq*.

A man? I looked back at Randa. We were both confused at their meaning.

It took us only an hour to find a suitable *abaaya*, veil and scarf; the selection seemed rather limited.

Life changed quickly. I had entered the *souq* area as an individual bursting with life, my face expressing my emotions to the world. I left the shopping area covered from head to toe, a faceless creature in black.

I must admit that the first few moments of veiling were exciting. I found the veil a novelty and looked back with interest as Saudi teenage boys stared at me, now a mysterious figure in black. I knew they were wishing for a bit of breeze to blow the veil away from my face so that they might catch a glimpse of my forbidden skin. For a moment, I felt myself a thing of beauty, a work so lovely that I must be covered to protect men from their uncontrollable desires.

The novelty of wearing the veil and *abaaya* was fleeting, though. When we walked out of the cool *souq* area into the blazing hot sun, I gasped for breath and sucked furiously through the sheer black fabric. The air tasted stale and dry as it filtered through the thin gauzy cloth. I had purchased the sheerest veil available, yet I felt I was seeing life through a thick screen. How could women see through veils made of a thicker fabric? The sky was no longer blue, the glow of the sun had dimmed; my heart plunged to my stomach when I realized that, from that moment, outside my own home I would not experience life as it really is in all its colour. The world suddenly seemed a dull place. And dangerous, too! I groped and stumbled along the pitted, cracked pavement, fearful of breaking an ankle or leg.

My friends burst out laughing at the awkwardness of my moves and my futile efforts to adjust my veil. I stumbled over several children of a bedouin woman, and looked in envy at the freedom of her veil. Bedouin women wear veils that fit across their noses, leaving their eyes free to examine their surroundings. Oh, how I wished to be a bedouin! I would cover my face gladly if I could only leave my eyes free to see the infinite changes of life around me.

We arrived early at the meeting-place designated by Omar. Randa glanced at her watch; we had nearly an hour before he was due. She suggested that we go back into the *souq* area since it was too hot in the boiling sun. Nadia and Wafa asked us if we wanted to have some fun. I said sure, without hesitation. Randa balanced from foot to foot, looking for Omar; I could tell she was uncomfortable with the very word *fun*. I, with my marvellous powers of persuasion, convinced Randa to go along with Nadia and Wafa. I was curious, never having broken any of the rules laid down for females. Poor Randa was simply accommodating to a stronger will.

The two girls exchanged smiles and told us to follow them. They made their way to a carpark beneath a new office building not far from the *souq* area. Men who worked in the building and nearby shops parked there.

We four young women inched our way across the busy intersection. Randa squealed and slapped my hand when I raised my veil so that I could see the traffic. Too late, I realized that I had exposed my face to every man on the street! The men appeared stunned by their luck, for they had seen a woman's face in a public place! I instantly realized it was far better for me to be run down by a speeding car than to commit such an act of revelation.

When we reached the carpark lifts, I staggered with shock at my friends' action. Wafa and Nadia approached a foreign man, a strikingly handsome Syrian. They asked him if he wanted to have some fun. For a moment, he seemed ready to bolt and run; he looked to his left and right and punched the lift button. Finally, he thought better of departing, considering the rare opportunity to meet available and possibly beautiful women in Saudi Arabia. He asked what kind of fun. Wafa asked the Syrian if he had a car and a private apartment. He said yes, he had an apartment and a room-mate, a Lebanese. Nadia asked if his friend was looking for a girlfriend, and the Syrian grinned and said, yes, indeed, both of them were.

Randa and I had recovered enough to move our feet. We gathered up our *abaayas* and ran out of the carpark in fear for our lives. In the process I lost my scarf; when I turned to pick it up, Randa ran straight into me. She fell backwards and lay sprawled in the sand, her forbidden legs exposed.

When Wafa and Nadia found us, we were breathing hard and leaning against a shop window. They were hanging on to each other, laughing. They had watched us earlier as I struggled to help Randa to her feet.

We whispered our angry words. How could they do such a stupid thing? Pick up foreign men! What kind of fun were they planning anyway? Didn't they know that Randa would be stoned and the three of us imprisoned, or worse? Fun was fun, but what they were doing was suicide!

Wafa and Nadia simply laughed and shrugged their shoulders at our outburst. They knew that if they were caught they would be punished, but they didn't care. To them, their impending future was so bleak it was worth a risk. Besides, they might meet a nice foreign man and marry him. Any man was better than a Saudi man!

I thought Randa was going to swoon. She ran into the street, looking up and down for Omar. She knew there would be no mercy from Father if she were caught in such a situation. She was terrified.

Omar, wary and perceptive, asked us what had happened. Randa fidgeted and started to speak, but I interrupted and told Omar a story about seeing a youth steal a necklace from the gold *souq*. He had been beaten by the shopkeeper and roughly hauled off to gaol by a policeman. My voice had a tremor as I told Omar we were upset because he was so young and we knew he would lose his hand for his act. I was relieved that Omar believed my story.

Randa inched her hand under my black cloak and gave me a squeeze of gratitude.

Later I found out from Nadia and Wafa what they called 'fun'. They met foreign men, usually from neighbouring Arab countries, occasionally a Brit or an American, in carpark lifts. They selected handsome men; men they felt they could love. Sometimes the men became frightened and jumped into the lift, zooming to another floor. At other times they would be interested. If the man they approached was intrigued, Wafa and Nadia would agree to a meeting-time, at the same lift. They would ask him to try to find a van, instead of a car, to pick them up. Later, at the agreed time, the girls would pretend to go shopping. Their driver would drop them at the *souq*; they would purchase a few items, and then go to the meeting-place. Sometimes the men would become wary and not show up; at other times they would be nervously waiting. If the men had obtained a van, the girls would make sure no-one was around and then jump quickly into the back. The men would cautiously drive to their apartment, and the same degree of caution would be used to smuggle the girls inside. If they were caught, the sentence would be severe, quite possibly death for everyone involved.

The explanation for the van was clear. In Saudi Arabia, men and women are not allowed in the same car unless they are close relatives. If the *mutawas* become suspicious, they will stop the vehicle and check identifications. Also, single men are not allowed to entertain women in their apartments or homes. At the slightest suspicion of impropriety, it is not uncommon for *mutawas* to surround the home of a foreigner and take everyone there, both male and female, to the gaol.

I was fearful for my friends. I warned them again and again of the consequences. They were young and reckless and bored with their lives. They laughingly told me of other activities they did for diversion. They dialled random phone numbers until a foreign man answered. Any man would do, so long as he was not Saudi or Yemeni. They would ask him if he was alone and longing for female companionship. Generally, the reply was yes since there are so few women allowed in Saudi Arabia and most foreign men work there on single-status visas. Once a man's eligibility was established, the girls would ask him to describe his body. Flattered, usually the man would graphically describe his body and then ask them to do the same. Then Wafa and Nadia would portray themselves from head to toe, in lewd detail. It was great amusement, they said, and they sometimes met the man later, in the same fashion as the carpark lovers.

I wondered how intimate my friends became with these pick-up lovers. I was astonished to hear that they did everything except penetration. They could not risk losing their virginity, for they realized the consequences they would face on their wedding night. Their husbands would return them to their homes, and their fathers would turn them away as well. The *mutawas* would investigate. They might lose their lives; if not, they would still have nowhere to live.

Wafa said that in their encounters with these men she and Nadia never removed their veils. They would take off all their clothes but keep their veils intact. The men would tease and beg and even try to force them to remove their veils, but the girls said they felt safe so long as no man saw their faces. They said if any of the men had become serious they might have considered exposing their faces. But, of course, none of them did. They, too, were only having fun. My friends were desperately trying to find an 'out' from their future, which loomed before them like a dark and endless night.

Randa and I wept when we discussed our friends' behaviour. I felt a hatred for the customs of my land creep into my throat like a foul taste. The absolute lack of control, of freedom for our sex, drove young girls like Wafa and Nadia to desperate acts. These were deeds that were sure to cost them their lives if they were discovered.

Before the year was out, Nadia and Wafa were arrested. Unfortunately for them, members of a self-proclaimed Public Morality Committee who roamed the streets of Riyadh in an effort to apprehend people in acts prohibited by the Koran had learned of their forbidden activities. Just as Nadia and Wafa entered the back of a van, a carload of young Saudi zealots wheeled in and blocked the vehicle. They had been watching the area for weeks after one of the committee members, while at work, overheard a Palestinian tell of two veiled women who propositioned him at the lift.

The lives of Wafa and Nadia were spared by the fact that their hymens were intact. Neither the Morals Committee nor the Religious Council, and especially not their fathers, believed their unlikely fabrication that they had simply asked the men for a ride when their driver was late. I suppose it was the best story they could concoct, considering the circumstances.

The Religious Council questioned every man who worked in the area and found a total of fourteen who said they had been approached by two veiled women. None of the men confessed that they had participated in any activities with them.

After three months of bleak imprisonment, owing to the lack of hard evidence of sexual activity the committee released Wafa and Nadia to their respective fathers for punishment.

Surprisingly, Wafa's father, the unbending man of religion, sat with his daughter and questioned her as to the reasons for her misdeeds. When she cried and told him her feelings of rejection and hopelessness, he expressed sorrow at her unhappiness. In spite of his regret and sympathy, he informed Wafa that it was his decision that she should be removed from all further temptations. She was advised to study the Koran and to accept a simple life preordained for women, far removed from the city. He arranged a hasty marriage with a bedouin *mutawa* from a small village. The man was fifty-three; and Wafa, seventeen, would be his third wife.

Ironically, it was Nadia's father who was gripped with a fearsome rage. He refused to speak with his daughter and ordered her confined to her room until a decision was made as to her punishment.

A few days later, my father came home early from the office and called Randa and me into his sitting-room. We sat disbelieving when he told us that Nadia was going to be drowned in her family's swimming-pool, by her father, on the following morning, Friday, at ten o'clock. Father said that Nadia's entire family would witness her execution.

My heart fluttered with fear when Father asked Randa if she or I had ever accompanied Wafa or Nadia on their shameful undertakings. I moved forward and started to voice my denials when Father shouted and shoved me back into the sofa. Randa burst into tears and told him the story of that day so long ago when we had purchased my first *abaaya* and veil. Father sat unmoving, eyes unblinking, until Randa had finished. He then asked us about our women's club, the one with the name of Lively Lips. He said that we might as well tell the truth, that Nadia had confessed all our activities days ago. When Randa's tongue froze, Father removed our club papers from his briefcase. He had searched my room and found our records and membership lists. For once in my life, my mouth was dry, my lips locked as with a chain.

Father calmly put the papers back into a pile on the briefcase. He looked clearly into Randa's eyes and said: 'On this day I have divorced you. Your father will send a driver within the hour to take you to your family. You are forbidden to contact my children.'

To my horror, Father turned slowly to me. 'You are my child. Your mother was a good woman. Even so, had you participated in these activities with Wafa and Nadia, I would uphold the teachings of the Koran and see you lowered into your grave. You will avoid my attention and concentrate on your schooling while I will work towards a suitable marriage.' He paused for a moment, coming close and looking hard into my eyes. 'Sultana, accept your future as one who obeys, for you have no alternative.'

Father stooped for the papers and his case and, without looking at Randa or me again, left the room.

Humiliated, I followed Randa to her room and numbly watched as she gathered her jewels, her clothes and her books into an unruly pile on the large bed. Her face was wiped clean of emotion. I could not form the words that were loose in my head. The doorbell rang too quickly, and I found myself helping the servants carry her things to the car. Without a word of farewell, Randa left my home, but not my heart.

At ten o'clock the next morning, I sat alone, staring yet unseeing out of my bedroom balcony. I thought of Nadia and imagined her bound in heavy chains, dark hood gathered around her head, hands lifting her from the ground and lowering her into the blue-green waters of her family swimming-pool. I closed my eyes and felt her body thrashing, her mouth gasping for air, lungs screaming for relief from the rushing water. I remembered her flashing brown eyes and her special way of lifting her chin while filling the room with laughter. I recalled the soft feel of her fair skin, and considered with a grimace the quick work of the cruel earth on such softness. I looked at my watch and saw that it was 10.10, and I felt my chest tighten with the knowledge that Nadia would laugh no more.

It was the most dramatic hour in my young history, yet I knew that my friends' schemes for fun, as bad or sad as they were, should not have caused Nadia's death or Wafa's premature marriage. Such cruel actions were the worst of all commentaries on the wisdom of the men who consume and destroy the lives and dreams of their women with emotionless indifference.

Chapter Nine

Foreign Women

After the sudden departure of Randa, the marriage of Wafa and the death of Nadia, I sank to the lowest possible level of existence. I can recall thinking that my body no longer required the fresh breath of life. I fancied myself in hibernation and wanted to feel the shallow breathing and lowered heartbeat experienced by creatures of the wild that will themselves away for months at a time. I would lie in my bed, hold my nose with my fingers, and pinch my mouth closed with my teeth. Only when my lungs forced the expulsion of air would I regretfully recognize that I had little control over my vital functions.

The house servants felt my pain keenly, for I was known as the sensitive member of our family and had always shown concern for their situation. The meagre amounts of cash doled out each month by Omar seemed a high price to pay for being so far removed from those they loved.

In an effort to rouse my interest in life, my Filipino maid, Marci, began to revive my thoughts by telling me stories of her country. Our long talks served to thaw the impersonal relationship that exists between mistress and servant.

One day she timidly revealed her life's ambition. She wanted to save enough money, working as a housemaid for our family, to return to the Philippines to study nursing. Filipino nurses are in great demand worldwide, and it is considered a lucrative career for women in the Philippines.

Marci said that after she graduated she would return to Saudi Arabia to work in one of our modern hospitals. She smiled as she reported that Filipino nurses made a salary of 3,800 Saudi riyals each month! Approximately $1,000 a month, compared to the $200 a month she earned as our maid. With such a large salary, she said, she could support her entire family in the Philippines.

When Marci was only three, her father was killed in a mining accident. Her mother was seven months pregnant with a second child. Their life was bleak, but Marci's grandmother tended to the two children while her mother worked two shifts as a maid in local hotels. Marci's mother repeated many times that knowledge was the only solution to poverty, and she frugally saved for her children's education.

Two years before Marci was to enrol in nursing school, her younger brother, Tony, was run over by a car and suffered extensive injuries. His legs were so crushed that they had to be amputated. His medical treatment ate away at Marci's school fund until the small tin can was bare.

Upon hearing Marci's life-story, I wept bitter tears. I asked her how she could maintain her happy smile day after day, week after week.

Marci smiled broadly. It was easy for her, she said, since she had a dream and a way to realize her dream.

Her experiences growing up in a wretchedly poor area in the Philippines left Marci feeling extremely fortunate to have a job and to fill her plate three times daily. People from her area did not actually die of hunger, she emphasized, but of malnutrition that left them vulnerable to diseases that would not have flourished in a healthy community.

Marci shared the stories of her people so vividly that I felt myself a part of her history, her land, her rich culture. I knew I had underestimated Marci and other Filipinos, for, until then, I had given them little thought other than to consider them simple folk lacking in ambition. How wrong I was!

Several weeks later Marci felt confident enough to talk about her friend Madeline. By telling me about Madeline, she opened up the question of the moral values of my land. Through Marci, I first learned that women from Third World countries were held as sex slaves in my own country, Saudi Arabia.

Marci and Madeline had been childhood friends. As poor as Marci's family was, Madeline's was poorer. Madeline and her seven siblings used to beg on the highway that connected their province to Manila. Occasionally, a big car transporting foreigners would stop and huge white hands would drop a few coins into their outstretched palms.

While Marci attended school, Madeline foraged for food.

At an early age, Madeline had a dream and a plan to bring that dream to reality. When she was eighteen, she sewed a dress from Marci's old school coat and travelled to Manila. There she located an agency that employed Filipinos to work abroad; Madeline applied for a maid's position. She was so petite and pretty that the Lebanese owner slyly hinted that he could get her a job in a Manila brothel; there she could earn a substantial amount beyond the imagination of a maid! Madeline, although raised in poor circumstances, was a devout Catholic; her negative reaction convinced the Lebanese that she would not sell her body. Sighing with regret, the man told her to fill in the application form and wait.

The Lebanese told her that he had just received a contract to supply more than three thousand Filipino workers to the Persian Gulf area, and that Madeline would be given priority in the maid positions since the rich Arabs always requested pretty maids. He winked and patted her on the buttocks as she left his office.

Madeline was both excited and frightened when she received confirmation of a maid's position in Riyadh, Saudi Arabia. About the same time, Marci's plans of attending nursing school fell through, and she decided to follow Madeline's footsteps and search for a job outside the Philippines. When Madeline left for Saudi Arabia, Marci joked that she would not be far behind. The good friends hugged their farewells and promised to write.

Four months later, when Marci learned that she, too, was to work in Saudi Arabia, she still had not heard from Madeline. Once there, she did not know where to find her friend, other than in the city of Riyadh. Since Marci was going to work for a family in the same city, she was determined to locate her friend.

I recall the night Marci arrived in our home. Mother was responsible for the running of the household and the placement of the servants. I remembered that Marci seemed a frightened little thing, immediately clinging to the eldest of our Filipino maids.

Since we had more than twenty servants in the villa, Marci was given little notice. As an inexperienced servant, only nineteen years old, she was assigned to clean the rooms of the two youngest daughters of the house, Sara and me. I had given her scant attention during the sixteen months she had patiently and quietly followed me through the villa, asking if I required anything.

Marci surprised me by confessing that other Filipino servants thought her blessed in her job since neither Sara nor I ever struck her or raised our voices in disapproval. My eyes flashed, and I asked Marci if people were struck in our home. I breathed a sigh of relief when she told me no, not in our villa. She did say that Ali was known to be difficult, always speaking in a loud and insulting tone. But his only violent action had been to kick Omar in the shin several times. I laughed, feeling little sympathy for Omar.

Marci whispered as she told me the gossip of the servants. She said that Father's second wife, a woman from one of the neighbouring Gulf states, pinched and beat her female servants daily. One poor girl from Pakistan had a brain injury from being knocked down the stairs. Told that she did not work fast enough, she rushed down to the washroom with a basket of dirty sheets and towels. When she accidentally bumped into Father's wife, the woman became so enraged that she punched the maid in the stomach, sending her tumbling down the stairs. As the girl lay moaning, the older woman ran down the stairs to kick and scream at the girl to finish her chores. When the girl did not move, she was accused of pretence. Eventually, the girl had to be taken to a doctor; she was still not normal, constantly holding her head in her hands and giggling.

Under orders from Father's wife, the palace doctor filled in a form stating that the girl had fallen and suffered concussion. As soon as she could travel, she was to be sent back to Pakistan. She was denied her past two months' salary and sent to her parents with only fifty Saudi riyals ($15).

Why did I act so surprised, Marci wanted to know. Most maids were mistreated in my country; our villa was a rare exception. I reminded her that I had been in many of my friends' homes and, while I had to admit that little consideration was given to servants, I had never witnessed an actual beating. I had seen some of my friends verbally abuse their maids, but I had paid it little heed since no-one had ever been physically assaulted.

Marci sighed wearily, and said that physical and sexual abuse were generally hidden. She reminded me that I live only yards from a palace that hid the sufferings of many young girls, and yet I had no knowledge of them. She softly told me to keep my eyes open, to observe how women from other lands were treated in my country. I nodded sadly in agreement.

Through this conversation, Marci became more aware of my empathetic nature. She decided to take me into her confidence and tell me the full story of her friend Madeline. I remember our conversation as well as if it were yesterday. Our exchanges are clear in my mind. I can see her earnest face before me now.

'Ma'am, I want you to know about my closest friend, Madeline. You are a princess. Perhaps the day will come that you can help us poor Filipino women.'

I was alone on that morning and felt boredom creeping into my day, so I nodded, eager for a morning of revealing gossip, even from a Filipino. I settled myself on my bed; Marci dutifully stuffed pillows behind my head, just the way she knew I liked them.

I told her: 'Before you begin your tale, go and get me a bowl of fresh fruit and a glass of *laban*.' (*Laban* is a buttermilk-like drink common in the Middle East.) After she had returned with a tray of fruit and my cold beverage, I stuck my feet out from under the covers and told Marci to rub them while she told me about this Madeline friend of hers.

Looking back, I burn with shame as I recall my selfish, childish manner. I was intrigued by the thought of a tragic story, yet not content to sit still and listen until all my desires were met! Older and wiser, now I can only look back with regret at the habits I picked up from my Saudi culture. No Saudi I know has ever shown the slightest interest in a servant's life: the number of family members; their dreams and aspirations. People from the Third World were there to serve us wealthy Saudis, nothing more. Even my mother, who was kind and loving, rarely expressed an interest in servants' personal problems; though I do attribute that to Mother's overwhelming responsibilities of running a huge household and also satisfying my demanding father. I had no such excuse. I cringe as I now acknowledge that Marci and the other servants were little more than robots to me, there to do my bidding. And to think that Marci and the household servants thought me kind, for I alone questioned them about their lives. It is a hard remembrance for one who considers herself sensitive.

Pensive, her face without expression, Marci began to rub my feet and started her story.

'Ma'am, before I left my country, I begged that Lebanese man for the address of Madeline's employer. He said no, he was not allowed. I told a lie, ma'am. I said that I had items to take to my friend from her mother. After I begged, he finally agreed, and gave me a phone number and the area of Riyadh that Madeline worked.'

'Is her employer a prince?'

'No, ma'am. He lives in the district called Al Malaz, about thirty minutes by car from here.'

Our palace was in the Al Nasiriyah area, a prestigious location inhabited by many royals, the most wealthy residential district of Riyadh. I had been in the area of Al Malaz once a long time ago and recalled many nice palaces of the upper business society of Saudis.

I knew Marci was forbidden to leave the palace grounds, other than on special monthly shopping trips organized by Omar for the female servants. Since our servants, like most domestics in Saudi Arabia, worked a brutal seven-day week, fifty-two weeks a year, I wondered how she could slip away to visit her friend.

I voiced my interest. 'How did you manage a trip to Al Malaz?'

Marci hesitated for a short moment. 'Well, ma'am, you know the Filipino driver Antoine?'

We had four drivers, two Filipinos and two Egyptians. I was generally driven by Omar or the other Egyptian. The Filipinos were used for grocery shopping and the running of errands. 'Antoine? The young one who is always smiling?'

'Yes, ma'am, that one. He and I like to see each other and he agreed to take me to find my friend.'

'Marci! You have a sweetheart!' I burst out

127

laughing. 'And Omar. How did you avoid getting into trouble with Omar?'

'We waited until Omar went with the family to Taif and we took our opportunity.' Marci smiled at my look of pleasure. She knew nothing gave me more joy than a successful trick pulled over the men of the household. 'First, I called the telephone number given to me in the Philippines. No-one would give me permission to speak with Madeline. I said I had a message from Madeline's mother. After a lot of hard work of convincing, I was told the location and description of the villa. Antoine drove to the area and located the place to deliver a letter to Madeline. A Yemeni took the letter from Antoine. Two weeks later I received a call from my friend. I could barely hear Madeline, for she whispered, afraid she would be discovered using the telephone. She told me she was in a very bad situation, please to come and help her. Over the telephone, we made a plan.'

I put aside my food and gave Marci my full attention. I told her to stop rubbing my feet. I felt the danger of their meeting and my interest in this brave Filipino whom I did not know grew.

'Two months passed. We knew the hot summer months would give us an opportunity to meet. We were afraid Madeline would be taken to Europe with her employer, but she was told to remain in Riyadh. When you and the family, along with Omar, left the city, I hid in the back seat of the black Mercedes and Antoine took me to Madeline.'

Marci, her voice cracking with her first show of emotion, described Madeline's dilemma: 'I sat in the car while Antoine rang the bell of the villa. While I was waiting, I could not help but notice the condition of the villa wall. The paint was peeling, the gate was rusty, the few bits of greenery hanging over the villa wall were dying from lack of water. I could tell it was a bad place. I knew my friend was in a dangerous situation if she worked in such a home.

'I felt depressed even before I was allowed inside. Antoine had to ring the bell four or five times before we heard activity as someone came to answer our call. Everything happened just as Madeline had said. It was creepy! An old Yemeni man dressed in a tartan wrap-around skirt opened the gate. He looked as though he had been sleeping; his ugly face told us he was none too happy at being awakened from a nap.

'Antoine and I both became frightened, and I heard the shaking of Antoine's voice when he asked, please, to speak to Miss Madeline from the Philippines. The Yemeni could hardly speak English, but Antoine has a little knowledge of Arabic. Together they managed to understand each other enough for the Yemeni to refuse us entry. He waved us away with his hand and began to close the door when I leaped from the back seat and began to cry. Through my tears, I told him that Madeline was my sister. I had just arrived in Riyadh and was working at the palace of one of the royal princes. I thought that might frighten him,

129

but his expression remained the same. I waved an envelope at him that had just arrived from the Philippines. Our mother was gravely ill. I had to speak with Madeline for a few moments to deliver a last message from our dying mother.

'I prayed to God not to punish me for such lies! I think God heard me, for the Yemeni seemed to change his mind when he heard the Arab word for *mother*. I saw that he was thinking. He looked first at Antoine and then at me, and finally told us to wait a moment. He closed the gate, and we heard the flip-flop of his sandals as he made his way back towards the villa.

'We knew the Yemeni was going inside to question Madeline and ask her to describe her sister. I looked at Antoine with a weak smile. It seemed our plan might work.'

Marci paused, remembering that day.

'Ma'am, that was a frightening Yemeni. He had a mean look and carried a curved knife at his waist. Antoine and I almost got in the car and drove back to the palace. But the thought of my poor friend gave me a feeling of power.

'Madeline had told me that two Yemenis guarded the villa. They watched the females of the house. None of the female servants was ever allowed to leave her place of work. Madeline had told me over the telephone that the young Yemeni was without a good heart and would not allow anyone in the gate, even a dying mother herself. Madeline thought we might succeed with the old Yemeni.

'Since the entire family was on holiday in Europe,

the young Yemeni had been given a two-week leave and had returned to Yemen to marry. At this time, the only men in the villa grounds were the old Yemeni and a gardener from Pakistan.

'I looked at my watch, and Antoine looked at his watch. Finally, we heard the shuffling of feet as the old man returned. The gate creaked with a slow swing. I shivered, for I had a feeling I was entering the gates of hell. The old Yemeni grunted and made a motion with his hands that Antoine was to stay outside with the car. Only I would be allowed inside.'

I tensed up as I imagined the fear Marci must have felt. 'How did you dare? I would have called the police!'

Marci shook her head. 'The police do not help Filipinos in this country. We would be reported to our employer and then gaoled or deported, according to the wishes of your father. The police in this country are for the strong, not for the weak.'

I knew what she said was true. Filipinos were a notch below us women. Even I, a princess, would never receive aid if it meant the police had to go against the wishes of the men of my family. But I did not want to think of my problems at that moment; I was wrapped up in Marci's adventure.

'Go on, tell me, what did you discover inside?' I imagined the inner workings of a Saudi Frankenstein's monster!

Having the full interest of her mistress, Marci became enlivened and began to make facial expressions and describe her experiences with relish.

'Following his slow steps, I was able to look all around. The concrete blocks had never been painted. A small block building nearby had no door, just an open space with a stringy old rag pulled across the top. Judging from the clutter of dirty mats, open cans and garbage smells, I knew the old Yemeni must live there. We walked by the family pool, but it was empty of water except for a black foul residue at the deepest end. Three tiny skeletons – which looked like the remains of baby kittens – were lying at the short end of the pool.'

'Kittens? Oh, my goodness!' Marci knew how I loved all baby animals. 'What a terrible death!'

'It looked like kittens. I guessed they were born in the empty pool and the mother cat was unable to get them out.'

I shuddered with despair.

Marci continued. 'The villa was large but had the same coarse look as the wall. Paint had been splashed on the blocks at some time in the past, but sandstorms had left it ugly. There was a garden, but the plants had all died from the lack of water. I saw four or five birds in a cage hanging under a large tree. They looked sad and skinny, without a song in their hearts to sing.

'Through the front door, the Yemeni yelled something in Arabic to an unseen person; he nodded his head at me and motioned for me to enter. I hesitated at the doorway as the bad-smelling air rushed over me. With great fear and trembling, I called out Madeline's name. The Yemeni turned and walked back to his interrupted sleep.

'Madeline came down a long dark hallway. The light was very dim, and after the bright sunshine outside I could barely see her walking towards me. She began to run when she saw it was really her old friend Marci. We rushed to embrace, and I was amazed to see that she was clean and smelled good. She was skinnier than when I last saw her, but alive!'

A feeling of relief flooded my body, for I had expected Marci to tell me she had found her friend half-dead, lying on a dirty mat, struggling to give her final instructions to take her body back to Manila.

'What happened then?' I was in a rush to discover the end to Marci's story.

Marci's voice took on the tone of a whisper, as though her memories were too painful to recall. 'After we completed our cries of greeting and our hugs, Madeline pushed me towards the long hallway. She held my hand and guided me to a small room off to the right. Directing me to a sofa, she sat on the floor facing me.

'She immediately burst into tears now that we were alone. As she buried her face in my lap, I stroked her hair and whispered for her to tell me what had happened to her. After she stopped her tears, she told me of her life since she had left Manila one year before.

'Madeline was met at the airport by two Yemeni servants. They were holding a card with her name spelled out in English. She accompanied the two men, for she did not know what else to do. She was alarmed at their wild appearance, and said she feared for her life as they careered through the city. It was late at night when she arrived at the villa; there was no light, so she did not notice the neglected grounds.

'At that time, the family was away at Makkah for the Haj pilgrimage. She was shown to her room by an old Arab woman who could not speak English. She was given biscuits and dates to eat and hot tea to drink. As the old woman left the room she handed Madeline a note that said she would be informed of her duties the following day.'

'The old woman must have been the grand-mother,' I said.

'Maybe – Madeline did not say. Anyhow, I do not know. Poor Madeline's heart sank when sunlight revealed her new home. She jumped at the sight of the bed in which she had slept, for the bedsheets were filthy; last night's glass and plate were swarming with cockroaches.

'With a sinking heart, Madeline located a bath-room only to discover the shower was not function-ing. She tried to cleanse herself in the sink with a remnant of dirty soap and tepid water. She wished in vain for God to calm her beating heart. Then the old woman knocked on the door.

'Having no choice, she followed the woman into the kitchen where she was handed a list of responsibilities. Madeline read the hastily scribbled note and saw that she was to assist the cook, be the housekeeper and care for the children. The old woman motioned for Madeline to prepare some food for herself. After eating breakfast, she began to scrub filth off the pots and pans.

'Along with Madeline, there were three other female employees: an old cook from India, an attractive maid from Sri Lanka and a plain maid from Bangladesh. The cook was at least sixty years old; the other two were in their mid-twenties.

'The cook refused conversation with anyone; she was returning to India within the next two months, and her dreams were of freedom and home. The plain maid was silent in her unhappiness, for her work contract had over a year until completion. The pretty maid from Sri Lanka did little work and spent most of her time in front of a mirror. She wished out loud for the return of the family. She hinted strongly to Madeline that she was much loved by the master of the house. She was expecting him to buy her a gold necklace upon his return from Makkah.

'Madeline said she was surprised when the pretty maid ordered her to turn around so she could see her figure. The maid then put her hands on her hips and declared with a grin that the master would find Madeline too skinny for his taste, but perhaps one of the sons would find her favourable. Madeline did not understand the implication and went on with her endless cleaning.

'Four days later, the family returned from Makkah. Madeline saw at once that her employers were of a low-class family; they were crude and ill-mannered, and their behaviour soon proved her assessment correct. They were accidentally wealthy without any effort on their part, and their only education was from the Koran, which in their ignorance they twisted to suit their needs.

'To the head of the household, the secondary status of women indicated in the Koran was understood to be slavery. Any woman who was not a Muslim was considered a prostitute. Matters were not helped by the fact that the father and two sons travelled to Thailand four times a year to visit the brothels in Bangkok and buy the sexual services of young beautiful Thai women. Knowing that some of the women of the Orient were for sale convinced the family that all women outside the Muslim faith were for purchase. When a maid was hired, it was assumed she was to be used like an animal, at the whim of the men of the house.

'Through the mother, Madeline immediately learned that she had been employed to serve as a sexual release for the two teenage sons. She informed Madeline that she was to serve Basel and Faris on an every-other-day basis. This information was given without emotion to Madeline's utter despair.

'To the surprise of the sexy maid, the father decided that Madeline was to his taste. He told his sons they could sleep with the new maid as soon as he had had his pleasure.'

I gasped and then held my breath; I knew what Marci was going to tell me. I did not want to hear it.

'Ma'am Sultana, that first night the family returned, the father raped Madeline!' She sobbed.

'That was only the beginning, for he decided that he liked her so much he continued to rape her on a daily basis!'

'Why did she not run away? Get someone to help her?'

'Ma'am, she did try. She begged the other servants to assist her! The old cook and the ugly maid did not wish to become involved and perhaps lose their salaries. The pretty maid hated Madeline, and said she was the reason she did not get her gold necklace. The wife and old woman were not treated well themselves by the master; they ignored her and said she was hired to please the men of the house!'

'I would have jumped out of a window and run away!'

'She tried to run away, many times. She was caught, and everyone in the house was ordered to guard her. Once, while everyone was sleeping, she went to the roof and dropped notes on the pavement begging for help. The notes were given to the Yemenis by some Saudi neighbours, and she was beaten!'

'What happened after you found her?'

Marci's face was sad and resigned as she continued. 'I tried many things. I called our embassy in Jeddah. I was told by the man that answered that they received many such complaints but there was little they could do. Our country relies on the money sent from workers abroad; our government did not want to antagonize the Saudi government by lodging formal complaints. Where would the poor Filipino people be without money from abroad?

'Antoine checked with some of the drivers about going to the police, but he was told the police would believe any story told by the Saudi employer and Madeline might get into a worse situation.'

I cried out: 'Marci! What could be worse?'

'Nothing, ma'am. Nothing. I did not know what to do. Antoine became frightened and said we could do nothing else. I finally wrote to Madeline's mother and told her of the situation, and she went to the employment agency in Manila and was told to go away. She went to our mayor in our town, and he said he was helpless. No-one wanted to get involved.'

'Where is your friend now?'

'I received a letter from her only a month ago. I am thankful she was sent back to the Philippines at the end of her two-year contract. Two new Filipinos, younger than Madeline, had replaced her. Can you believe, ma'am, Madeline was angry at me? She thought I had left her without trying to help.

'Please believe that I did all that I could. I wrote her a letter and explained all that happened. I have not received a reply.'

I could not say a word in defence of my country-men. I stared into Marci's face, at a loss.

She finally broke the silence. 'And that, ma'am, is what happened to my friend in this country.'

I could tell Marci was heartbroken for her friend. I myself was stricken with sorrow. How does a person respond to such a tale of horror? I could not. In shame at the men of my country, I no longer felt superior to the young girl who only moments before was my servant, my inferior. Engulfed by remorse, I buried my head in my pillow and dismissed Marci with a flick of my hand. For many days, I was quiet and withdrawn; I thought of the myriad accounts of abuse that torture the minds of the people, both Saudis and foreigners, living in this land I call my home.

How many more Madelines are there, reaching out to uncaring souls and discovering the nothingness that is dressed in the official uniform of those paid to care? And the men of the Philippines, Marci's land, were little better than the men of my country, for they fled from personal involvement.

When I awoke from my unsettling sleep of mortification, I began to interrogate my friends and ferret out their passivity regarding the fate of their female servants. Through my tenacity, I was inundated with firsthand accounts of unspeakable and vile acts committed by men of my culture against women from all nations.

I heard of Shakuntale from India, who at the age of thirteen was sold by her family for a sum of 600 Saudi riyals ($170). She was worked by day and abused by night in much the same manner as the unsuspecting Madeline. But Shakuntale had been bought. She was property that would not be returned – Shakuntale could never go home again. She was the property of her tormentors.

I listened in horror as a mother laughingly

dismissed the plight of her Thai maid who was raped at will by the son of the house. She said that her son needed sex, and that the sanctity of Saudi women forced the family to provide him with his own woman. Oriental women do not care whom they go to bed with, she stated with assurance. Boys are kings in the eyes of their mothers.

Suddenly aware of pervasive evil, I asked Ali why he and father travelled to Thailand and the Philippines three times a year. He scowled and told me it was none of my business. But I knew the answer, for many of the brothers and fathers of my friends made the same trek to the beautiful lands that sold their young girls and women to any beast with money.

I discovered that I had known little about men and their sexual appetites. The surface of life is nothing more than a façade; with little effort I uncovered the evil that lurks under the thin crust of civility between the sexes.

I, for the first time in my young life, comprehended the impossible task facing those of our sex. I knew my goal of female equality was hopeless, for I finally recognized that the world of men harbours a morbid condition of overfondness for themselves. We women are vassals, and the walls of our prisons are unscalable for this grotesque disease of pre-eminence lives in the sperm of all men and is passed along, generation to generation – a deadly incurable disease whose host is male and victim is female.

Ownership of my body and soul would soon

pass from my father to a stranger I would call my husband, for Father had informed me I would be wed three months after my sixteenth birthday. I felt the chains of tradition wrap tightly around me; I had only six short months of freedom left to savour. I waited for my destiny to unfold, a child as helpless as an insect trapped in a wicked web not of its making.

Chapter Ten

Huda

It was ten o'clock at night on 12 January 1972, and all nine of my sisters and I were spellbound with the telling of Sara's future by our old Sudanese slave, Huda. Since Sara's traumatic marriage and divorce, she had taken to studying astrology and was convinced that the moon and stars had played a determining role in her life's path. Huda, who had filled our ears from an early age with stories of black magic, was pleased to be the centre of attention and to provide distractions from the sameness of life in dull Riyadh.

We all knew that Huda, in 1899, at the age of eight, after straying from her mother who was busy digging yams for the family supper, had been captured by Arab slave-traders. In our youth she had entertained the children of the house for countless hours with the saga of her capture and confinement.

Much to our merriment, Huda always re-enacted her capture with great flair, no matter how many times she retold the story. She would crouch by the sofa and sing softly, pretending to scratch in the sand. With a wild screech, she would yank a pillow cover from behind her back and pull it over her head, gasping and kicking against her imagined tormentors. She would moan and fling herself to the floor and kick and scream for her mother. Finally, she would leap on to the coffee-table and peer out of the sitting-room windows, describing the blue waters of the Red Sea from the ship that transported her from Sudan to the deserts of Arabia.

Her eyes would grow wild as she fought imaginary thieves for her small portion of food. She would snatch a peach or a pear from the fruit-bowl and hungrily gobble all but the stone. Then she would march solemnly around the room, hands behind her back, chanting to Allah for deliverance as she was led to the slave-market.

Sold for a rifle to a member of the Rasheed clan of Riyadh, she stumbled as she was led from the streets of Jeddah through blinding sandstorms to the Mismaak fortress, the garrison for the Rasheed clan in the capital city.

Now, in her re-enactment, Huda lurched from one piece of furniture to another. We would squeal with laughter as Huda leaped around the room dodging bullets from our kin, the young Abdul Aziz and his sixty men, as they attacked the garrison and defeated the Rasheeds, reclaiming the country for the Al Sa'ud clan. She would throw her fat body over a chair and scramble for cover as the desert warriors slew their enemies. She told of her rescue by my father's father and would end her playacting by wrestling the nearest one to the floor and kissing her repeatedly as she swore she kissed our grandfather upon her rescue. This is how Huda came to be in our family.

As we grew older, she diverted us from our various dramas by frightening us with supernatural claims of sorcery. Mother used to dismiss Huda's proclamations with a smile, but after I woke up screaming about witches and potions she forbade Huda to divulge her beliefs to the younger children. Now that Mother was no longer with us, Huda returned to her former habit with gusto.

We watched with fascination as Huda peered at the lines running across Sara's palm and squinted her beady black eyes as though she saw Sara's life unfolding before her like a vision.

Sara seemed scarcely affected, as though she expected those very words, as Huda solemnly told her she would fail to realize her life's ambitions. I groaned and leaned back on my heels; I so wanted Sara to find the happiness she deserved that I found myself irritated with Huda and loudly dismissed her prophecies as the mumbo-jumbo I wanted them to be. No-one paid me any heed as Huda continued to scrutinize Sara's lifelines. The old woman rubbed her bony chin with her hand and muttered: 'H'm, little Sara. I see here that you will marry soon.'

Sara gasped and jerked her hand from Huda's grasp. The nightmare of another marriage was not what she wanted to hear.

Huda laughed softly and told Sara not to run from her future. She added that Sara would know a marriage of love and would grace the land with six small ones who would give her great joy.

Sara gathered her brow in a worried knot. Then she shrugged her shoulders and dismissed what she could not control. She looked my way and gave a rare smile. She asked Huda to read my palm, saying that if Huda could foretell what actions her unpredictable baby sister would take, then she, Sara, would be a believer in Huda's powers until the end of time. My other sisters rocked with laughter as they agreed with Sara, but I could tell by their looks that they loved me with a fierce tenderness, their little sister who so tried their patience.

I lifted my head with a haughtiness I did not feel as I plopped myself down in front of Huda. I turned my palms up and demanded, in a loud and bossy manner, to know what I would be doing one year from that date.

Huda ignored my youthful rudeness and studied my upturned palm for what seemed like hours before announcing my fate. She surprised us all with her posturings; she shook her head, muttered to herself and groaned aloud as she pondered my future. Finally, she fixed her eyes on my face and uttered her soothsaying with such confidence that I feared her forecast and felt the sinister hot wind of magic in the words she spoke.

In a freakish deep-throated voice, Huda pronounced that Father would soon inform me of my upcoming marriage. I would find misery and happiness in one man. I would rain destruction on those around me. My future actions would

145

bring good along with bad to the family I loved. I would be the beneficiary of great love and dark hate. I was a force of good and evil. I was an enigma to all who loved me.

With a piercing cry, Huda threw her hands in the air and asked Allah to intervene in my life and protect me from myself. She unseated me as she lunged towards me and wrapped her arms around my neck and began to lament in a wild high-pitched howl.

Nura jumped to her feet and rescued me from Huda's smothering grasp. My sisters comforted me as Nura led Huda from the room, mumbling under her breath for Allah to protect the youngest daughter of her beloved Fadeela.

I was shivering from the impact of Huda's prediction. I began to sob and blurted out that Huda had bragged to me once about being a witch, that her mother had been a witch before her and the power had flowed from her mother's milk into the suckling infant that was Huda. Indeed, I moaned, only a witch could recognize such a one as evil as I!

Tahani, one of my older sisters, told me to hush, a silly game had gone awry and there was no need for dramatics. Sara, in an attempt to lighten the mood, brushed my tears away and said my sorrows were based on the worry that I could never live up to Huda's wild predictions. Joining in Sara's efforts, my other sisters began to joke and recalled with great peals of laughter some of the capers I had successfully pulled on Ali over the years. They reminded me of one of their favourites, which in our camaraderie we began to tell again.

The caper began when I asked one of my girl-friends to call Ali and pretend to be smitten with his charms. For hours we had listened in as he babbled nonsense on the telephone and made elaborate plans to be met by the girl's driver behind a nearby villa under construction.

The girl convinced Ali he must be holding a baby goat on a lead so that her driver could identify him. She told him that her parents were out of town; it was safe for Ali to follow the driver to her home for a secret meeting.

The building-site was across the street from my girlfriend's home, and my sisters and I had joined her on her bedroom balcony. We made ourselves sick with laughter as we watched poor Ali stand for hours, holding on to the baby goat and stretching his neck for signs of the driver. Much to our amusement, the girl managed to talk Ali into the same situation not once, not twice, but on three occasions! In Ali's eagerness to meet a girl, he had lost his sanity. I remember thinking that this silly veiling business works both ways!

Encouraged by my sisters' laughter and confidence, I managed to put Huda's rumblings out of my mind. After all, she was over eighty years of age, and was more than likely senile.

My consternation returned with a rush when Father visited us that evening and announced that he had found a suitable husband for me. With a sinking heart I could only think that the first of

Huda's predictions had come true. In my terror, I failed to ask Father the name of my husband-to-be and fled the room with darkness in my eyes and bile in my throat. I lay awake most of the night and thought of Huda's words. For the first time in my young life, I feared my future.

Nura returned to our villa the following morning to advise me that I was to wed Kareem, one of the royal cousins. As a young child, I had played with this cousin's sister, but recalled little she had said about him other than that he was a bossy brother. He was now twenty-eight years of age, and I was to be his first wife. Nura told me that she had seen a photo of him; he was exceptionally handsome. Not only that; he had been educated in London as a lawyer. Even more unusual, he had distinguished himself from most of the royal cousins in that he held a real position in the business world. Recently, he had opened his own large law firm in Riyadh. Nura added that I was a very lucky girl, for Kareem had already told Father that he wanted me to complete my schooling before starting a family. He did not want a woman with whom he could not share mental exchanges.

In no mood to be patronized, I made an ugly face at my sister and pulled the bedcovers over my head. Nura drew a long breath when I shouted out that I was not the lucky one; instead my cousin Kareem was the one with luck!

After Nura left, I called Kareem's sister, whom I knew slightly, and told her to advise her brother that he had best reconsider marrying me. I threatened that if we married he could not take other wives or I would poison them all at my first opportunity. Besides, I told her, Father had had a difficult time finding a husband for me since I had had an accident in the school lab. When Kareem's sister asked me what had happened, I pretended to be shy but finally admitted that I had stupidly dropped a flask of acid; as a result my face was hideously scarred. I had a good laugh when she hung up the phone in a rush to tell her brother.

Later that evening, Father stamped furiously into the villa with two of Kareem's aunties in tow. I was forced to stand at attention while they looked me over for any signs of facial scars or misshapen limbs. I became so angry at the examination that I opened my mouth and told them to check my teeth, if they dared. I leaned towards them and made loud chomping sounds. Looking back over their shoulders in dismay, they ran out of the room when I neighed like a horse and raised the bottoms of my feet to their faces, which is a terrible insult in the Arab world.

Father stood and looked at me for a long moment. He seemed to be battling his emotions; and then, to my complete astonishment, he shook his head and began to laugh. I had fully expected a slap or a lecture – never in my wildest imagination did I expect him to laugh. I felt a trembling smile form on my face, and then I, too, began to convulse with laughter. Curious, Sara and Ali came into the room and stood, with questioning smiles on their faces.

Father collapsed on the sofa, wiping tears off his face with the hem of his *thobe*. He looked at me and said: 'Sultana, did you see their faces when you tried to bite them? One looked like a horse herself! Child, you are a wonder. I do not know whether to pity or envy your cousin Kareem.' Father blew his nose. 'For sure, life with you will be a tempestuous affair.'

Feeling heady with my father's approval, I sat on the floor and leaned across his lap. I wanted to hold the moment for ever when he squeezed my shoulders and smiled down at his amusing daughter. Taking advantage of the intimate scene, I became brave and asked Father if I could meet Kareem before the wedding.

Father turned and looked at Sara; something in her expression touched his heart. He patted the sofa beside him and asked her to sit. There were no spoken words among the three of us, but we communicated through the bond of generations.

Ali, stunned at the attention given to the females in the family, leaned against the door-frame with his mouth in a perfect circle; he was struck dumb.

Chapter Eleven

Kareem

Much to father's amazement, and to my bitter disappointment, Kareem's family did not break off our engagement. Instead, Kareem and his father arrived at Father's office the following week and politely asked that Kareem be allowed to meet me – under proper supervision, of course. Kareem had heard of my unorthodox behaviour with his relatives and was decidedly curious to discover if I were completely mad or just high-spirited.

Father had not responded to my earlier entreaty to meet Kareem, but a request from the man's family was a different matter. After discussing the issue at length with several of the family aunties and my sister Nura, Father gave a favourable reply to Kareem's request.

Wild with joy, I danced around the room when Father told me the news. I was going to meet the man I would marry before I married him! My sisters and I were electrified, for it was just not done in our society; we were prisoners who felt the ever-present chains of tradition lighten.

Kareem's parents and my father and Nura decreed that Kareem and his mother would come to our villa in two weeks' time for afternoon tea.

Kareem and I would be chaperoned by Nura, Sara, two of my aunties and his mother.

With this possibility of control of my life on the horizon, hope was born, a fantasy I dared not imagine only yesterday. I found myself excited and wondered if I would find Kareem to my taste. Then I was struck with a new and unpleasant thought: perhaps Kareem would not like me! Oh, how I wanted to be beautiful like Sara, so that men's hearts would throb with desire.

Now I stood for hours gazing in the mirror – cursing my small stature, twisting my short unruly curls. My nose seemed too small for my face, my eyes had no lustre. Perhaps it was best to hide me under a veil until the night of the wedding!

Sara chuckled at my agony and tried to reassure me: men loved petite women, particularly ones with small upturned noses and smiling eyes. Nura, whose opinion everyone respected, said laughingly that I was considered very pretty by all the women in the family. I had just never pursued beauty; perhaps the time had come for me to enhance my assets.

Suddenly consumed with yearnings to be considered a desirable woman, I told Father I had nothing to wear. For, even though we Saudi women veil on the streets, our dark coverings are discarded the moment we enter the home of a female friend. Since we cannot awe those of the opposite sex, other than our husbands, with our carefully selected fashions, we females attempt to dazzle each other. Here, we really do dress for other women!

For instance, women in my country will arrive at an afternoon tea-party carefully dressed in lace and satin, with their garments tastefully accented by a display of priceless diamonds and rubies.

Many of my foreign friends have been stunned by the plunging necklines and skimpy clothing hidden under our dowdy *abaayas*. I have been told that we Saudi women resemble bright exotic birds with our choice of attire under our black veils and *abaayas*. Without a doubt, we women in black take more time and effort with our individual clothing under our cloaks than do Western women, who are free to flaunt their fashionable clothes.

Father, delighted that I was displaying an interest in a marriage he had thought I would disrupt, easily gave in to my pleas. Nura and her husband travelled with me to London for a three-day shopping spree at Harrods. I took great pains to tell the Harrods salesladies that I was going to meet my fiancé the following week. Just because I was a Saudi princess, I did not want them to assume I was without choices in my life. I felt disappointed that no-one expressed awe or surprise at my proud announcement. Those who are free cannot fathom the value of small victories for those who live on a tether.

While in London, Nura arranged for me to have a cosmetic makeover and a wardrobe colour chart prepared. When told that emerald green was my most flattering shade, I bought seventeen outfits in that one colour. My unruly hair was pulled back in a smooth twist and I stared in delicious wonder at the sophisticated stranger in the shop windows as I walked through the shopping districts in London.

Sara and Marci helped me dress on the day of the party. I alternately cried and cursed at the impossibility of duplicating my London hairstyle when Huda suddenly appeared at my bedroom door. 'Beware,' she cried, her eyes narrowing to slits. 'First you will know happiness, but then unhappiness will come with your new husband.' I threw my hairbrush at her and loudly told her not to spoil my day with her gibberish. Sara twisted my ear and told me to be ashamed of myself; Huda was just an old woman. My conscience did not hurt me at all, and I told Sara so. Sara replied that the reason was that I did not have a conscience. We sulked with each other until the gate-bell rang; then she hugged me and said I looked lovely in my emerald-green dress.

I was actually going to see my future husband in the flesh! The sound of my pounding heart filled my ears. Feeling all eyes on me watching for my reaction made me blush, which was ruining the sophisticated entrance I had planned. Oh, to return to the safety of my childhood!

I had no need for such emotions. Not only was Kareem the most handsome man I had ever seen; his sensuous eyes caressed my every move and made me feel quite the loveliest creature on earth. Within minutes of our strained introduction, I knew he would never call off our engagement. I discovered in myself a surprising hidden talent, one that is most helpful to women who must manipulate to achieve their goals. I learned I was a natural flirt. With the greatest of ease I found myself pursing my lips and looking at Kareem through lowered lids. My imagination soared: Kareem was only *one* of my many suitors.

Kareem's mother was watching me closely, in obvious distress at my vampish mannerisms. Sara, Nura and my aunties were exchanging pained looks. But Kareem was hypnotized, and nothing else mattered.

Before Kareem and his mother left, he asked if he could call me one evening later in the week to discuss our wedding plans. I scandalized my aunties by failing to ask their permission first and replied: 'Of course. Any time after nine would be all right.' I gave Kareem a woman's smile of promise when he said goodbye.

I hummed my favourite tune, a Lebanese love-ballad, as Nura, Sara and my aunties told me in great detail every wrong move I had made. They declared that Kareem's mother was sure to insist the wedding be called off, since I had practically seduced her son with my eyes and lips. I told them they were just all jealous because I had the chance to see my husband before the wedding. I stuck my tongue out at my aunties and told them they were too old to understand the beatings of young hearts; I left them standing wide-eyed in shock at my audacity. Then I locked myself in my bathroom and began to sing at the top of my lungs.

Later I thought about my performance. Had I not liked Kareem, I would have ensured that he not like me. I liked him, so I willed him to fall in love. My actions had been well thought out: if I had found him repulsive and wanted our engagement cancelled, I would have eaten without any manners, belched in his mother's face, and spilt hot tea in his lap. If Kareem and his family were still not convinced that I was an unworthy wife for Kareem, I had thought I might break wind. Luckily for Kareem and his mother, they were saved from a shocking afternoon since I had found him attractive and pleasing in character. I was so relieved to know I would not be marrying an old man blunted from life that I thought love would find fertile ground in our union.

With such pleasant thoughts in my mind, I gave Marci six pretty outfits from my wardrobe and told her I was going to ask Father if she could go with me to my new home.

Kareem called me that night. With a great deal of amusement, he told me his mother had advised him against our marriage. She had quivered in fury at my boldness and predicted I would bring heartache to her eldest son and, in turn, disaster to the entire family.

Feeling confident in my newly found female wiles, I tartly replied that he had best consider his mother's advice.

Kareem whispered that I was the girl of his dreams: a royal cousin, bright and of good humour. He declared he could not abide the women his mother wanted him to wed; they sat fixed like stones, and he knew they tried to anticipate his every wish. He liked a woman with spunk; he would be bored with the ordinary. He added, in a sexy murmur, that I made his eyes happy.

Kareem then brought up a puzzling subject; he asked if I had been circumcised. I told him I would have to ask Father. He cautioned me: 'No, do not ask. If you do not know, then that means you were not.' He seemed pleased with my reply.

In my innocence, I blurted out the question of circumcision at the dinner-table. It was Father's turn with his third wife on that particular evening, so Ali was sitting at the head of the table. Aghast at my question, he put his glass down with a thump and looked to Sara for comment. I continued to scoop my bread into the dish of houmous, and for a moment failed to see the anxiety in the eyes of my sisters. When I looked up, I saw that everyone was ill at ease.

Ali, thinking himself the leader of the family, banged his fist on the table and demanded to know where I had heard the word. Realizing something was amiss, I remembered Kareem's warning and said I had overheard some of the servants talking.

Ali dismissed my ignorance with a glare in my direction and curtly told Sara to call Nura in the morning and have her speak to 'this child'.

With our mother now dead, Nura, as the eldest, was responsible for my knowledge of such subjects. She arrived at the villa before ten o'clock the next morning and came directly to my room. She had been summoned by Ali. She made a wry face when she said that Ali had informed her that her performance as eldest daughter was sadly lacking. He, Ali, intended to notify Father of his observations and displeasure.

Nura sat on the edge of the bed and asked me in a kind voice what I knew of the relations between a man and a woman. I replied confidently that I knew all there was to know.

My sister smiled as she spoke. 'I fear that your tongue is your master, little sister. Perhaps you do not know all of life.'

As she discovered, I knew plenty about the *act* of sex.

In Saudi Arabia, as in much of the Arab world, the subject of sex is considered taboo. As a result, women talk of little else. Discussions regarding sex, men and children dominate all female gatherings.

In my country, with so few activities to soothe women's minds, the main occupation for women is to gather in each other's palaces. It is not un-common to attend a women's party each day of the week, excluding Fridays, which is our religious day. We gather, drink coffee and tea, eat sweets, lounge on overstuffed sofas and gossip. Once a woman begins to veil, she is automatically included in these functions.

Since my veiling, I had listened in fascination as young brides told of their wedding night; no detail was too intimate to reveal. Some of the young women shocked the female gatherings by declaring that they enjoyed sex. Others said they pretended to enjoy their husbands' advances, to keep them from taking another wife. Then there were those women who so despised sex that they kept their eyes closed and endured the assaults of their husbands with dread and repulsion. Significantly, there were a few who remained silent during such discussions and shied away from the topic; those were the women who were dealt with in a cruel manner by the men in their lives, much in the same way that Sara had been brutalized.

Nura, convinced that I understood the implications of marital life, added little to my awareness. She did disclose that it was my duty, as a wife, to be available to Kareem at all times, no matter my feelings at the moment. I proclaimed that I would do as I willed, that Kareem could not force me against my inclinations. Nura shook her head. Neither Kareem nor any other man would accept refusal. The marriage bed was his right. I stated that Kareem would be different. He would never use force. Nura said that no man was understanding about such matters. I should not expect it, or I would be crushed with disappointment.

To change the subject, I asked my sister about circumcision. Her voice thin and low, Nura told me that she had been circumcised when she was about twelve years old. She said the rite had been performed on the three sisters that followed her in age. The youngest six daughters of our family had been spared the barbaric custom owing to the intervention of a Western physician who spoke for many hours against the ritual with our father. Nura added that I was blessed not to have endured such a trauma.

I could see that my sister was close to tears; I asked her what had happened.

For more generations than Nura knew, the women of our family had been circumcised. Our mother, like most Saudi women, was circumcised when she became a woman, a few weeks before she was wed. At the age of fourteen, when Nura became a woman, Mother followed the only tradition she knew and arranged for Nura's circumcision to be performed in a small village some miles from Riyadh.

A celebration was held, a feast prepared. A youthful Nura basked in the attention bestowed upon the one of honour. Moments before the rite, Nura was told by Mother that the elder women were going to perform a small ceremony, and that it was important for Nura to lie very still. One woman beat a drum, other women chanted. The oldest women gathered around the frightened child. Nura, nude from the waist down, was held by four women on a bedsheet that had been spread on the ground. The oldest of the women raised her hand in the air; with horror Nura saw that she had a razor-like instrument in her hand. Nura screamed. She felt a sharp pain in her genital region. Dizzy with shock, she was lifted in the air by the women and congratulated on her coming of age. Thoroughly frightened, she saw blood pouring from her wounds. She was carried into a tent and her lacerations were dressed and bandaged.

Her wounds healed quickly, but she did not understand the implication of the procedure until her wedding night; there was unbearable pain and much blood. As the condition persisted, she grew to dread sex with her new husband. Finally, after becoming pregnant, she saw a Western doctor who was appalled at her scars. He told Nura that her entire external genitalia had been removed and that, for sure, the sex act would always result in tearing, pain and bleeding.

When the physician discovered that three more of Nura's sisters had been circumcised and that the remaining six would more than likely suffer the same consequences, he pleaded with her to arrange for her parents to visit him in his clinic.

My other three sisters visited the physician. He said our sister Baher was in much worse condition than Nura, and he did not know how she endured sexual relations with her husband. Nura had been a witness to our sisters' ceremonies and recalled that Baher had fought the old women and had actually managed to run a few yards from her tormentors. But she was caught and returned to the mat, where her struggles caused much mayhem and a great loss of blood.

To the doctor's surprise, it was my mother who had insisted upon the circumcision of her daughters. She herself had endured the rite; she was certain it was the will of Allah. Finally, the physician convinced our father of the utter nonsense of the procedure, as well as of the health risks. Nura said I had been saved from a custom that was cruel and useless.

I asked Nura why she thought Kareem would

enquire of such a matter. Nura said I was fortunate that he was a man of the opinion that it was good for a woman to be complete. She said that many men still insisted upon circumcision of their brides. It was all a matter of the region you were from or the opinion of the family in which a girl was born. Some families continued the practice while others left it in the barbaric past, where it belonged. Nura said it sounded to her like Kareem wanted a wife who would share pleasure, not just be an object of pleasure.

Nura left me with my thoughts. I knew I was lucky to be one of the younger females in our family. I shuddered when I imagined the trauma Nura and my other sisters had endured.

I was glad Kareem was concerned for my welfare. I was beginning to entertain the notion that some women might be happy in my land, in spite of traditions that do not belong in a civilized society. But still the unfairness of it all lingered in my thoughts. We women of Arabia could find happiness only if the man ruling us was considerate; otherwise, sorrow would surround us. No matter what we do, our future is linked to one prerequisite: the degree of kindness in the man who rules us.

Feeling drowsy, I went back to sleep; I dreamed I was in a beautiful emerald-green wedding-gown waiting for my groom, Kareem. He failed to arrive, and my dream turned into a nightmare and I awoke in a trembling sweat; I was being pursued by ghoulish old women in black, razors in hand, screeching for my blood.

I cried out for Marci to bring me cold water. I was in anguish, for I recognized the meaning of my frightening vision: a major obstacle to change and relief from our antiquated customs was the women of Arabia themselves. The women of my mother's generation were uneducated, and had little knowledge other than what their men told them to be true; as a tragic result, such traditions as circumcision were kept alive by the very people who had themselves suffered under the cruel knife of barbarism. In their confusion of past and present, they were unwittingly strengthening the men in their efforts to keep us in ignorance and seclusion. Even when told of the medical dangers, my mother had clung to the traditional past; she could imagine no other path for her daughters than the one she herself had trod, for fear that any shift from tradition would harm their marriage chances.

Only we modern educated women could change the course of women's lives. It was in our power, within our wombs. I looked to my wedding date with determined anticipation. I would be the first of the Saudi women to reform her inner circle. It would be my sons and daughters who would remodel Arabia into a country worthy of all its citizens, both male and female.

Chapter Twelve

The Wedding

On the occasion of my wedding, the preparation room was filled with gaiety. I was surrounded by women of my family; no one person could be heard, for all were speaking and laughing as a singular and grand celebration.

I was in the palace of Nura and Ahmed, which had been completed only a few weeks before my wedding date. Nura was pleased with the outcome and was anxious for word of her gilded mansion to leak throughout the city of Riyadh and cause all to exclaim at the money spent and the glory accomplished.

I myself hated Nura's new palace; for romantic reasons, I had wanted to be wed in Jeddah, by the sea. But my father had insisted upon a traditional wedding; and I, for once, made no outcry when my demands were not met. I had decided months ago to hold back my passion except for matters of paramount importance and to let little irritations slide easily away. Doubtless I was becoming exhausted with the disabilities of my land.

While Nura beamed happily, our female relatives were heaping compliments upon the beauty of the palace. Sara and I exchanged small smiles, for we had agreed some time ago that the palace was in the worst possible taste.

Nura's marble palace was enormous. Hundreds of Filipino, Thai and Yemeni labourers, supervised by unsmiling German contractors, had worked around the clock for months to create the monstrosity. The painters, the woodworkers, the metalworkers and the architects did not speak with one voice; as a result, the palace conflicted within itself.

The halls were gilded and richly adorned. Sara and I counted 180 paintings hanging in the entry-hall alone. Sara recoiled in dismay and said that the works of art had been picked by one with little or no knowledge of the great masters. Garish carpets with embroidered birds and beasts of every type laid across endless floors. The ornate bedrooms made my soul feel heavy; I wondered how children of the same blood could so differ in judgement of style.

While Nura had failed miserably in decorating her home, her gardens were a masterpiece. Nearly a mile of lakes and lawns decorated with beautifully arranged flowers, shrubs and trees encircled her palace. There were many surprises to delight the eye: sculptures, colourful bird-houses, fountains spouting water, and even a children's merry-go-round.

I was going to be married to Kareem in the garden at nine o'clock in the evening. Nura knew that I loved yellow roses, and thousands of them, flown in from Europe, were now floating on the lake beside the rose-covered pavilion where Kareem would come to claim me. Nura proudly announced that people were already whispering that this was the wedding of the decade.

There are no announcements of engagements and weddings in Saudi Arabia; these matters are considered extremely private. But gossip of money spent and grand occasions staged travels throughout the land, with each section of the royal family striving to outspend the other.

I slapped at my aunties and screamed when the hair on my private parts was so rudely removed. Yelping in pain, I asked where such a savage custom had begun. My oldest aunty slapped my face for such impudence. She looked hard into my eyes and announced that I, Sultana, was a stupid child and that as a daughter of the Muslim faith I should know that the Prophet recommended, for the sake of cleanliness, that all pubic and armpit hair should be removed every forty days. I, wilful as ever, shouted that the practice no longer made sense; after all, modern Muslims are equipped with hot water and soap to wash away our dirt. We no longer had to use the sand of the desert for such purposes!

My aunty, knowing the futility of arguing with me, continued with her duties. I shocked all present when I loudly proclaimed that, if the Prophet could speak in this new age of modern amenities, I knew he would end such a silly tradition. Certainly, I announced loudly, this one issue alone proved that we Saudis were like uninspired mules; we trod the same weary track as the mule before us even if it led us to plunge off a cliff. Only when we evolved as spirited stallions, with a strong will of our own, would we progress and leave the era of those primitives behind us.

My relatives exchanged worried glances, for they lived in dread of my rebellious spirit and felt comfortable only with complacent women. My contentment with the one chosen for my husband was considered nothing less than miraculous, but until the final ceremony was complete none of my relatives would breathe easily.

My dress was made of the brightest red lace I could find. I was a bold bride, and I took great delight in scandalizing my family, who had begged me to wear a soft peach or pale pink instead. As was my way, I refused to relent. I knew I was right. Even my sisters finally admitted that my skin and eyes were flattered by the bright colour.

I was in a happy daze when Sara and Nura lowered the dress over my head and shoulders and fastened the delicate buttons around my waist.

A moment of sadness came as Nura draped Kareem's gift of rubies and diamonds around my neck. I could not escape the image of my mother on the sad day of Sara's wedding when I had sat as a child on the floor and watched her fasten the unwanted jewels around the neck of Sara. It had been only two short years ago, yet it seemed another life, another Sultana. I shed my gloom and smiled when I realized Mother must be watching me from a great distance with a satisfied glow in her eyes. I could barely breathe in the tight bodice as I leaned down to pick up a bouquet of spring flowers made entirely of precious stones, especially designed for the occasion by Sara.

Looking into my sisters' smiling faces, I announced: 'I am ready.'

It was time for my new beginning, another life.

The beating of the drums drowned out the orchestra imported from Egypt. With Nura on one side and Sara on the other, I made my proud appearance to the expectant guests, waiting impatiently in the garden.

As with all Saudi weddings, the official ceremony had been conducted earlier. With Kareem and his family in one part of the palace and I and my family in another, the religious sheikh had gone from room to room, asking us if we accepted the other. Kareem and I had not been allowed to say our words of promise in the other's presence.

For four days and nights our family had been celebrating. The celebration would continue another three days and nights after our appearance before our female guests. Tonight's ceremony was merely a stage created for the lovers to bask in the beauty of observance of youth and hope. Our night of glory.

I had not seen Kareem since the day of our first meeting. Our courtship had continued, none the less, by long hours of playful telephone conversation. Now I watched Kareem, escorted by his father, walk slowly towards the pavilion. He was so handsome, and he was going to be my husband.

For some odd reason, I was fascinated with the beating of his heart. I watched the tremor of movement in his throat and counted the beats. My imagination swept me into his chest, to that powerful spot of romance, and I thought: This heart is mine. I alone have the power to make it beat with happiness or with misery. It was a sobering moment for a young girl.

Finally, he stood tall and straight before me; I was suddenly overcome with emotion. I felt my lips tremble and my eyes water as I fought against the urge to weep. When Kareem removed my face-cover, we both burst out laughing, our emotion and joy were so intense. The audience of women began to applaud loudly and stamp their feet. In Saudi Arabia it is rare that a bride and groom find such obvious pleasure in each other.

I was drowning in Kareem's eyes, and he in mine. I was overcome with the emotion of disbelief. I had been a child of darkness, and my new husband, instead of being the expected object of dread, was sweet freedom from the misery of my youth.

Anxious to be alone, we lingered only a short while after the ceremony to receive the congratulations of our female friends and relatives. Kareem threw gold coins from small velvet bags towards various groups of merry guests while I slipped away to change into travelling clothes.

I wanted to speak with my father, but he had hurried from the garden the moment his role was complete. His mind was relieved; his youngest and most troublesome daughter of his first wife was now safely wed and no longer his responsibility. I ached with the desire for a bond between us that had been in my dreams but never broke into reality.

For our honeymoon, Kareem had promised me we would go anywhere and do anything I desired. My every wish was his command. With the glee of a child, I listed all the places I wanted to see and all the things I wanted to do. Our first stop would be Cairo, and from there on to Paris, New York, Los Angeles and then Hawaii. We would have eight precious weeks of freedom from the scars of Arabia.

Dressed in an emerald-green silk suit, I hugged my sisters goodbye. Sara was weeping so violently that she could not bear to turn me loose. She kept whispering, 'Be brave,' and my heart broke for my sister; I understood too well that the remembrances of her wedding night would never disappear. With the passing of years, perhaps the thoughts of her honeymoon would merely fade away.

I covered my designer suit with the black *abaaya* and veil and snuggled in the back seat of the Mercedes with my new husband. My fourteen bags had already been taken to the airport.

For the sake of privacy, Kareem had purchased all the first-class seats on each flight of our trip. The Lebanese air hostesses wore bright smiles as they watched our silly behaviour. We were as adolescents, for we had never learned the art of courtship.

Finally, we arrived in Cairo, rushed through Customs, and were driven to an opulent villa on the banks of the ancient Nile. The villa, which belonged to Kareem's father, had been built in the eighteenth century by a rich Turkish merchant. Restored by Kareem's father to its original splendour, the villa was laid out in thirty rooms on irregular levels with arched windows leading to the lush garden. The walls were covered with delicate dusty-blue tiles, with intricate carved creatures in the background. I felt seduced by the house itself. I told a proud Kareem that it was a wonderful setting in which to begin a marriage.

The impeccably decorated villa brought the garish decorating defects of Nura's palace to mind. I suddenly realized that money did not automatically bestow artistic discrimination on those of my country, even in my own family.

I was only sixteen, still a child, but my husband understood the implications of my youth, and he eased my introduction into the world of adults with a unique solution. He, as I, disagreed with the manner of marriage in our land. He said that strangers should not be intimate, even if those strangers were husband and wife. In his opinion, men and women should have time to understand the secrets of the other that make desire grow. Kareem told me that he had decided weeks before that he and I would have our courtship after our marriage. And, when I was ready for him, I would be the one to say: 'I want to know all of you.'

We spent our days and nights playing. We

dined, rode horses around the pyramids, browsed through the crowded bazaars of Cairo, read books and talked. The servants were puzzled at such a joyous couple who chastely kissed good night and went into separate bedrooms.

On the fourth night, I pulled my husband into my bed. Afterwards, with my drowsy head on Kareem's shoulder, I whispered that I would be one of the scandalous young wives of Riyadh who cheerfully admitted I enjoyed sex with my husband.

I had never been to America and was anxious to form an opinion of the people who spread their culture worldwide yet seemed to know so little of the world themselves. New Yorkers, with their pushy rude manners, frightened me. I was happy when we arrived in Los Angeles, with its pleasant relaxed ambience which feels more familiar to Arabs.

In California, after weeks of meeting transported Americans from practically every state in the Union, I announced to Kareem that I liked these strange loud people, the Americans. When he asked me why, I had difficulty in voicing what I felt in my heart. I finally said: 'I believe this marvellous mixture of cultures has brought civilization closer to reality than in any other culture in history.' I was certain Kareem did not understand what I meant and I tried to explain. 'So few countries manage complete freedom for all their citizens without chaos; this has been accomplished in this huge land. It appears impossible for large numbers of people to stay on a course of freedom for all when so many options are available. Just imagine what would happen in the Arab world; a country the size of America would have a war a minute, with each man certain he had the only correct answer for the good of all! In our lands, men look no farther than their own noses for a solution. Here, it is different.'

Kareem looked at me in amazement. Not used to a woman interested in the greater scheme of things, he questioned me into the night to learn my thoughts on various matters. It was obvious that my husband was not accustomed to a woman with opinions of her own. He seemed in utter shock that I thought of political issues and the state of the world. Finally, he kissed me on the neck and said that I would continue my education once we returned to Riyadh.

Irritated at his tone of permission, I told him I was not aware that my education was up for discussion.

The planned eight-week honeymoon turned into ten weeks. Only after a call from Kareem's father did we reluctantly drag ourselves back to our families. We planned to live in the palace of Kareem's father and mother until our own palace was built.

I knew that Kareem's mother looked upon me with distaste; now it was in her power to make my life miserable. I thought of my foolish disregard for tradition, which had brought about her scorn, and cursed myself for thinking so little of my future by alienating my mother-in-law at our first meeting. I knew that Kareem, like all Arab men, would never side with his wife against his mother. It would be up to me to arrive with an olive branch extended in peace.

I had an unpleasant shock as the plane prepared to land in Riyadh. Kareem reminded me of my veil. I scrambled to cover myself in black and felt a fierce longing for the sweet scent of freedom that had begun to fade the moment we entered Saudi airspace.

With the tightness of dread in my throat, we entered his mother's palace to begin our married life. At that moment, I was unaware that Kareem's mother so disliked me that she had already begun plotting ways to bring our happy union to an end.

Chapter Thirteen

Married Life

If there could be one word that would describe the Saudi women of my mother's generation, it would be *waiting*. They spent their lives waiting. Females of that era were banned from education and job opportunities, so there was little to do but wait to be married, wait to give birth, wait for grandchildren and wait to grow old.

In Arab lands, age brings great satisfaction for women, for honour is bestowed upon those women who fulfil their productive duties with many sons and therefore ensure the continued lineage of the family name.

My mother-in-law, Noorah, had spent her life waiting for a daughter-in-law to bestow the honour she felt was now her due. Kareem was her eldest child, the most beloved son. Saudi customs of the old days demanded that the wife of the firstborn son do his mother's bidding. Like all young women, I knew of this tradition, but reality tends to fade from my thoughts until the time I must confront the facts.

Certainly, desire for male children is common in much of the world; but no place can compare with Arab lands, where every woman must endure boiling tension throughout her childbearing years, waiting for the birth of a son. Sons are the sole reason for marriage, the key to satisfaction for the husband. Male children are so treasured that a fierce bond develops between mother and son. Nothing, other than the love of another woman, can separate the two. From the moment we were wed, Kareem's mother thought of me as her competitor, not as a welcome member of the family. I was the promise of a wedge between Noorah and her son; my presence only intensified her pervasive mood of general unhappiness. Some years before, her life had taken an abrupt turn that had poisoned her outlook.

The first wife of Kareem's father, Noorah had borne her husband seven living children, three of whom were sons. When Kareem was fourteen, his father had taken a second wife, a Lebanese woman of great beauty and charm. From that moment, there had been no peace within the walls surrounding the palaces of the two wives.

Noorah, a mean-spirited woman, was positively malevolent over her husband's second marriage. In her hate, she was driven to consult a sorcerer from Ethiopia – who served the palace of the king but was for hire to the other royals – and paid him a great sum to put a curse on the Lebanese woman so that she would be barren. Noorah, proud of her own productivity, was convinced that the Lebanese would be divorced if she could not produce sons.

As it turned out, Kareem's father loved the Lebanese woman and told her he did not care whether she gave him children. As the years passed, it became evident to Noorah that the Lebanese was not going to give birth or be divorced. Since the greatest driving force in Noorah's life was to rid her husband of his second wife, she consulted the sorcerer and paid an even larger sum to bring a cloud of death upon the Lebanese.

When Kareem's father heard the idle gossip of Noorah's scheming at the palace, he came to her in a rage. He swore that if the Lebanese woman died before Noorah he would divorce Noorah. She would be sent away in disgrace and forbidden contact with her children.

Noorah, convinced that the barren womb was a result of the sorcerer's power, was now terrified that the woman would die; surely black magic was unalterable. Since that time, Noorah was obliged to protect the Lebanese woman. She now spent an unhappy life trying to save the life of the very woman she had tried to kill by voodoo.

It was a strange household.

In her unhappiness, Noorah lashed out at those around her, excluding her children. Since I was not of her blood and was greatly loved by Kareem, I was her natural target. Her intense jealousy was evident to everyone except Kareem, who, like most sons, saw little wrong in his devoted mother. In her maturity, she had apparently gained wisdom, for she made a great pretence of affection to me – when Kareem was within hearing distance.

Each morning I happily walked Kareem to the gate. Hard at work at his law firm, he would leave by nine, which is early for anyone, particularly a prince, to begin work in Saudi Arabia. Few members of the royal family arise before ten or eleven.

I was certain Noorah watched us from her bedroom window, for the moment the gate closed behind him Noorah would begin to call my name with the greatest urgency. None of the thirty-three servants employed in her household would do; she would cry out for me to serve her hot tea.

Since I had spent my childhood mistreated by the men of my family, I was in no mood to spend the second part of my life abused by women, even Kareem's mother.

For the present, I remained mute. But Kareem's mother was soon to learn that I had faced antagonists much more fierce than an old woman with dark mental recesses. Besides, there is an old Arab proverb that says: 'Patience is the key to solutions.' In an attempt to exchange success for failure, I thought it best to heed the wisdom passed down from generations. I would be patient and await an opportunity to reduce Noorah's power over me.

Fortunately, I had little time to wait. Kareem's younger brother, Muneer, had recently returned from his studies in America. His anger at being back in Saudi Arabia bit deeply into the peace of the household.

Although much has been written about the enforced monotony of women's lives in Saudi Arabia, scant attention has been given to the wasted lives of many of our young men. True, their lives are bliss compared with those of women; still, much is lacking, and the young men of Arabia spend many languid hours longing for stimulation. There are no cinemas, clubs or mixed dining since men and women are not allowed in restaurants together unless they are husband and wife, brother and sister, or father and daughter.

Muneer, only twenty-two years old and accustomed to the freedoms of American society, did not relish his return to Saudi Arabia. He had recently graduated from business school in Washington DC, and had plans to be a liaison for government contracts. While waiting for his opportunity to prove his adeptness in acquiring huge sums of money – a passion with all the royal princes – he began to keep company with a group of princes within the family known for their risky behaviour. They gave and attended mixed parties. Foreign women of questionable morals who worked for the various hospitals and airlines were in attendance.

Drugs were abundant. Many of these princes had become addicted to alcohol, drugs, or both. In their drug- or alcohol-induced haze, their dissatisfaction with their kin who ruled the land festered. Not content with modernization, they longed for Westernization; these young men were ardent for revolution. Not surprisingly, their idleness bred dangerous talk and conduct, and before long their revolutionary intrigues were common knowledge.

King Faisal, once a carefree youth himself who was transformed into a pious king, diligently followed the actions of his young kin and attempted, in his solicitous manner, to guide the young men of the family from the excesses of empty lives. Some of the troublesome princes were placed in the family business while others were sent off to the military.

After King Faisal spoke of his concern about Muneer's unseemly behaviour to his father, I heard loud shouting and angry voices from the study. I, like the other female members of the family, soon found some urgent task in the map room, directly opposite the study. With eyes on the maps and ears tuned to the shouting, we gasped when we heard Muneer accuse the ruling family of corruption and waste. Muneer swore that he and his friends would bring the changes so direly needed in the kingdom. With curses on his lips and a call for rebellion, he stormed out of the villa.

While Muneer claimed the country needed to move into the future, his commitment was vague and his real activities troubling. His was a sad tale of misjudgement; alcohol and easy money had seduced him.

Few foreigners today are aware that alcohol was not banned to non-believers (non-Muslims) in the Kingdom of Saudi Arabia prior to 1952. Two separate and tragic events involving royal princes brought about the ban by our first king, Abdul Aziz.

In the late 1940s, Prince Nasir, the son of our ruler, returned from the United States a different man from the one who had departed the kingdom. He had discovered the enticement of the combination of alcohol and uninhibited Western women.

In his assessment, alcohol was the key to idolization by women.

Since Nasir held the position of governor of Riyadh, he found few barriers to his desire to maintain secret supplies of alcohol. Nasir held forbidden parties, entertaining men as well as women. In the summer of 1947, after a late-night gathering, seven of the partakers died from drinking wood alcohol. Some of the dead were women.

Nasir's father, King Abdul Aziz, became so incensed at this needless tragedy that he personally beat his son and ordered him to gaol.

Later, in 1951, when Mishari, another son of the king, while intoxicated shot and killed the British vice-consul and almost killed the man's wife, the old king's patience expired. From that time forward, alcohol was banned in the Kingdom of Saudi Arabia and black-marketing schemes were born.

The people of Saudi Arabia react to the prohibited much in the same manner as people of other cultures. The forbidden becomes even more enticing. Most Saudi men and women I know drink socially; a large number have acquired serious addiction to the substance. I have never been in a Saudi home that did not have a large assortment of the finest and most expensive alcoholic beverages to offer to guests.

Since 1952, the cost of alcohol had risen to 650 Saudi riyals for a bottle of Scotch ($200). A fortune could be made in importing and selling the illegal drink. Since Muneer and two cousins who were high-ranking princes were of the opinion that alcohol should be legalized, they combined their energies and soon became fabulously wealthy transporting illegal alcohol from Jordan.

When border guards became suspicious of the cargo, they were paid off. The only obstacle to the illegal importing of alcohol is the ever-roving bands of the Committees for the Propagation of Virtue and the Prevention of Vice. These committees were formed by the *mutawas*, religious men who tremble in anger at the effrontery of members of the Saudi royal family who, above all others, are presumed to uphold Islamic law yet prove time and again that they consider themselves above the teachings of the Prophet.

One of these committees soon was Muneer's undoing and unwittingly provided the solution to my obtrusive mother-in-law.

It was a Saturday, our first day of the week (Muslims celebrate their religion on Fridays), a day none of Kareem's family will ever forget.

Kareem sullenly walked through the doorway, weary from a hot trying day at his office, and came upon his mother and wife in a rough shoving match. When she saw her son, Noorah widened the twilight war with her new daughter-in-law by sobbing and loudly proclaiming to Kareem that I, Sultana, was filled with disrespect for his mother, and that for no apparent reason I had started the brawl with her.

As she fled the scene she pinched me on the forearm, and I, in a widening mood of anger, rushed after her and would have taken a swing at her but for Kareem's intervention. Noorah looked hard at me and turned to Kareem. She hinted darkly that I was an unfit wife, and that if he investigated my activities he would be prompted to divorce me.

Any other day Kareem might have laughed at our ridiculous and infantile display, for women with little but time on their hands tend to manoeuvre themselves into numerous squabbles. But on that day he had been informed by his London broker that over the previous week he had lost more than a million dollars on the stock market. In his black mood, he rushed to meet violence with a vengeance. Since no Arab man will ever contradict his mother, Kareem slapped me three times across the face. They were slaps meant to insult, since they accomplished little more than to redden my jaw.

My strong character was formed by the age of five. I have the tendency to be nervous at the sight of trouble looming. As the danger draws near, I become less nervous. When the peril is at hand, I swell with ferocity. As I grapple with my assailant, I am without fear and fight to the finish with little thought of injury.

The battle was on. I swung at Kareem with a rare and priceless vase that just happened to be nearby. He saved his face by a quick move to the left. The vase shattered as it struck a Monet painting worth hundreds of thousands of dollars. The vase and the water-lily painting were destroyed. In a fine fury,

I grabbed an expensive oriental ivory sculpture and threw it at Kareem's head.

The crashing and banging, along with our shouts, alerted the household. Women and servants burst suddenly upon us with loud cries. By this time, Kareem realized I was going to destroy the room, which was filled with his father's beloved treasures. To stop me, he punched me in the jaw. Inky darkness surrounded me.

When I opened my eyes, Marci was standing above me, dripping cold water on my face from a soaking cloth. I heard loud voices in the background and assumed that the excitement over my fight with Kareem was continuing.

Marci said no, the new disturbance concerned Muneer. Kareem's father had been summoned by King Faisal regarding a container of alcohol that had leaked the illegal substance in a trail down the streets of Riyadh. The Egyptian driver had stopped at a shop for a sandwich, and the pervasive smell of alcohol had caused a crowd to gather. Detained by a member of one of the committees to prevent vice, he, in his fear, had volunteered the name of Muneer and one other prince. The head of the Religious Council had been alerted and he had contacted the king. The king was in a rare rage.

Kareem and his father left the villa to return to the king's palace. The drivers were sent in search of Muneer. I nursed my swollen jaw and plotted a new plan of revenge on Noorah. I could hear her cries of grief; I gathered myself and walked down the circular staircase, sniffing the air for her sobs.

I, a woman far removed from sainthood, wanted to see and feel the full pleasure of her distress. I followed her cries to the sitting-room. I would have smiled but for my painful jaw. Noorah was crumpled in a corner of the sitting-room, crying out for Allah to save her beloved Muneer from the wrath of the king and the men of religion.

Noorah saw me and instantly quietened. After long moments of silence, she looked at me with contempt and said: 'Kareem has promised me he will divorce you. He agrees that "Who grows up on a habit will die with it" [Arab proverb], and you have grown up wild. There is no place for such a one as you in this family.'

Noorah, expecting tears and pleas, which are common from those deemed helpless, searched my face closely when I replied that I myself was going to demand a divorce from her son. I declared that Marci was at that very moment packing my bags; I would leave her oppressive home within the hour. As an added insult, I called over my shoulder that I was going to influence my father into calling for Muneer to be made an example for those who so disdain the laws of our faith. Her precious son would more than likely be flogged or gaoled, or both. I left Noorah with her jaw hanging in fear.

The tables had turned. My voice rang with a confidence I did not feel. Noorah had no way of knowing if I possessed the behind-the-scenes power that could accomplish my threats. She would celebrate if her son divorced me; she would be mortified if I were the one to seek a divorce. It is difficult, but not impossible, for a woman in Arabia to divorce her husband. Since my father was a prince closer in blood to our first king than Kareem's father, Noorah had a moment of fear that I could be successful in my claim to call for Muneer's punishment. She had no knowledge that my father would more than likely turn me out of our home for my imprudence, and that I would have nowhere to turn.

Appropriate actions to follow my bold threats were required. When Marci and I appeared at the door loaded with travelling-cases, the household broke open like an explosion.

By coincidence, Muneer, located at the home of a friend and ordered home, had just arrived with one of the drivers. Unaware of the seriousness of his predicament, he swore when I informed him that his mother had brought about the pending divorce of her eldest son.

A wave of perverse optimism swept through my body as Noorah, incited to action by the possibility of my vociferous wrath, insisted I not leave the house. The double crisis had impaired Noorah's resolve; she emerged thoroughly weakened in our bitter feud. After much pleading on her part, I reluctantly remained.

I was sleeping when Kareem returned, exhausted from an evening of mortification. I overheard his appeal to Muneer to consider the name of their father before committing acts that were forbidden. I did not have to strain to hear Muneer's insolent response, accusing Kareem of helping to oil the mammoth machine of hypocrisy that was the Kingdom of Saudi Arabia.

King Faisal was revered by most Saudis for his dedicated and devout style of life. Within the family itself, he was held in deep respect by the elder princes. He had led our country from the dark days of King Sa'ud's rule into a position of regard and even admiration from some quarters. But there was a deep divergence between the elder princes and the younger princes within the family.

Devoured by desire for unearned wealth, these young men of the family hated the king, who cut their allowances, prohibited their entry into illegal businesses, and chided them when they strayed from the path of honour. There was not even a flicker of compromise between the two camps, and trouble continuously brewed.

That night, Kareem slept a great distance from me in our large bed. I heard him through the night as he tossed and turned. I knew he was plunged in dark thoughts. I had a rare touch of guilt as I pondered the severity of his troubles. I decided that if my marriage survived that day's grievous wounds I would temper my attitude.

The next morning, a new Kareem emerged. He failed to speak or acknowledge my presence. My good intentions of the previous night vanished into the pale morning light. I told him in a loud voice that I thought a divorce best. In my heart I longed for him to appeal for peace.

He looked at me and replied in a dry frightening voice: 'Whatever you think, but we will settle our differences when this family crisis is behind us.' Kareem continued to shave, as if I had said nothing out of the ordinary.

This new foe, indifference, quietened me and I sat, humming a tune, as one unconcerned, while Kareem finished his dressing. He opened the bedroom door and left me with this parting thought: 'Sultana, you know, you deceived me with your warrior's spirit, hidden behind the smile of a woman.'

After he had departed, I lay in the bed and sobbed until I was exhausted.

Noorah coaxed me to the table of peace, and we settled our differences with gestures of love. She sent one of her drivers to the jewellery *souq* to purchase a diamond necklace for me. I hurriedly travelled to the gold *souq* and purchased the most expensive gold breastplate necklace I could find. I spent more than 300,000 Saudi riyals ($80,000) and cared little what Kareem would say. Now I saw the possibility of peace with a woman who could cause me endless grief should my marriage be saved.

Weeks passed before Muneer's fate was decided. Once again, the family saw no benefit in publicizing the misadventures of the royal sons. The wrath of the king was somewhat tempered by the efforts of my father and various princes who sought to downplay the incident as one of a foolish young man recently influenced by the evils of the West.

Noorah, thinking that I had somehow influenced my father, was grateful and responded by exclamations of the joy in her heart for having such a one as I as her daughter-in-law. The truth was never revealed: that I spoke not a word to my father. His interest stemmed from the very real fact that I was married into the family and he did not desire association with Kareem's brother should a scandal arise. His concern was for himself and Ali. Even so, I was thoroughly pleased at the outcome and was a heroine, admittedly undeservedly, in my mother-in-law's eyes.

Once again, the *mutawas* were quietened by the king's efforts. King Faisal was held in such high esteem by the Religious Council that his appeals were heard and heeded.

Muneer was brought into his father's business and sent to Jeddah to manage the new offices. To buy off his discontent, he was awarded large government contracts. Within a few months, he told his father he wanted to wed, and a suitable cousin was found and his happiness increased. Within months he began to gain weight and joined the ranks of the royal princes who live for making more and more money until their bank accounts overflow and produce enough income from the interest to rival the budgets of small countries.

Kareem had moved into a separate bedroom the day of our conversation. Nothing his mother or father could say or do persuaded him to reconsider our decision to divorce.

Much to my horror, one week after our estrangement, I discovered I was pregnant. After much soul-searching, I decided I had no option but to abort my pregnancy. I knew that Kareem would never agree to a divorce if he discovered I was with child. But one such as I had no use for a husband under duress.

I was in a dilemma, for abortions are not common in my land – many children are desired by most – and I did not have the slightest clue where to go and whom to see.

My investigation was delicate. Finally, I entrusted my secret to a royal cousin who informed me that her younger sister had become pregnant the year before while on holiday in Nice. She had been unaware of her condition and returned to Riyadh. Her fear of her father finding out was such that she had attempted suicide. The mother had shielded the daughter's secret and had located an Indian physician who, for excessive fees, performed abortions for Saudi women. I carefully planned my escape from the palace to the offices of the abortionist. Marci was my confidante.

I was waiting, despondent, in the physician's office when a red-faced Kareem burst through the door. I was a veiled woman among other veiled women, but he recognized me by my unusual silk *abaaya* and my red Italian-made shoes. He pulled and pushed me through the door, screaming to the receptionist that the office had best be closed immediately for he, Kareem, was going to see the doctor in prison.

I was smiling beneath my veil and in the best of tempers as Kareem alternately professed his love for me and cursed me. He glittered and he glared! He cast away my fears of losing him as he vowed that he had never considered divorce; his stance was merely a combination of pride and anger.

Kareem had discovered my plan when Marci divulged the secret to another maid in the house. This maid had gone to Noorah, and my mother-in-law had frantically located Kareem in the office of a client and hysterically reported that I was going to kill her unborn grandchild.

Our child was saved by mere moments. I would have to reward Marci.

Kareem herded me into the house with curses. In our room he covered me with kisses and we wept and made our peace. It had taken a series of mishaps to lead us to our peak of happiness.

Miraculously, all had ended well.

Chapter Fourteen

Birth

The most complete and powerful expression of life is birth. The acts of conceiving and giving birth are more profound and beautiful than any miracle of art. This I learned as I waited for our first child with such great joy and happiness.

Kareem and I had meticulously planned the birth. No detail was too small to take into account. We made reservations to travel to Europe four months before the expected date of arrival. I would give birth at Guy's Hospital in London.

As with so many carefully laid plans, minor occurrences prevented our departure. Kareem's mother, blinded by a new veil made of thicker fabric than usual, sprained her ankle when she stumbled over an old bedouin woman sitting in the *souq*; a close cousin on the verge of signing an important contract requested that Kareem postpone his departure; and my sister Nura frightened the family with what the doctor thought was an appendicitis attack.

Once we were past these crises, false labour pains began. My physician forbade me to travel. Kareem and I accepted the inevitable and set about making arrangements for our child to be born in Riyadh.

Unfortunately, the King Faisal Specialist Hospital and Research Centre that would offer us royals the latest medical care had yet to open. I would give birth at a smaller institution in the city, best-known for harbouring germs and for its lackadaisical staff.

Since we were of the royal family, we had options not available to other Saudis. Kareem arranged for three rooms in the maternity ward to be converted into a royal suite. He hired local carpenters and painters. Interior decorators from London were flown in, tape measures and fabric samples in hand.

My sisters and I were guided through the unit by the proud hospital administrator. The suite glowed a heavenly blue with silk bedcovers and curtains. An elaborate baby-bed with matching silk coverlets was fastened with heavy bolts to the floor, in case a member of the negligent staff should carelessly tip the bed and toss our precious child to the floor! Nura bent double with laughter when told of the precaution and warned me that Kareem would drive the family insane with his schemes to protect our child.

I sat speechless when Kareem advised me that a staff of six would soon arrive from London to assist me in the birth. A well-known London obstetrician, along with five highly skilled nurses, had been paid an enormous fee to travel to Riyadh three weeks prior to the estimated delivery date.

Since I was a motherless child, Sara moved into the palace towards the end of my pregnancy. She watched me as I watched her. I observed her carefully, absorbing the sad changes in my dear sister. I told Kareem I feared she would never recover from her abhorrent marriage; her quiet moods were now a permanent component of what had once been a thoroughly cheerful and joyous character.

How unfair life could be! I, by my very aggressiveness, could have better dealt with an abusive husband, for bullies tend to be less forceful in the face of someone who will stand up to them. Sara, with her peaceful soul and gentle spirit, had been an easy target for the arrogance of her untamed husband.

But I was thankful for her smooth presence. As my body swelled, I became jittery and unpredictable. Kareem, in his excitement over fatherhood, had lost all his good sense.

Owing to the presence of Kareem's brother Asad and various cousins who came and went at will, Sara had been careful to veil when she left our apartments on the second floor. The single men of the family were housed in another wing, but they roamed the palace at all hours. After Sara's third day in our home, Noorah sent word through Kareem that there was no need for her to veil when she entered the main living-areas of the villa or the gardens. I was pleased for any loosening of the tight restraints on women that so encumbered our lives. Sara was apprehensive in the beginning, but soon shed the excess covering of black with ease.

One evening, late, Sara and I were reclining in wicker loungers, enjoying the cool night air of the common garden. (There are women's gardens and common or family gardens in most Saudi palace grounds.) Unexpectedly, Asad and four acquaintances returned from a late-night appointment.

When she heard the men approaching, Sara turned her face to the wall, for she had no desire to bring disgrace on the family by showing herself to strangers. I felt no inclination to emulate her movement, so I loudly proclaimed our presence by shouting to Asad that there were unveiled women in the garden. The men with Asad hurriedly passed our way without a glance and entered one of the side-doors to the men's sitting-room. As a courtesy, Asad casually walked our way to speak and enquire of Kareem's whereabouts – and his eyes happened to rest on Sara's face.

His physical reaction was so sudden that I feared he had been stricken with a heart attack. His body jerked so grotesquely that I moved as rapidly as my belly allowed and shook his arm to get his attention. I was genuinely concerned. Was he ill? Asad's face was flushed, and he seemed unable to move without direction; I led him to a chair and called out loudly for one of the servants to bring water.

When no-one responded, Sara jumped to her feet and rushed inside to get the water herself. Asad, embarrassed, tried to leave, but I was convinced that he was about to faint. I insisted he stay. He said he felt no pain, yet he could not explain his sudden loss of movement.

Sara returned with a glass and a bottle of cold mineral water. Without looking at him, she poured a drink and raised the glass to his lips. Asad's hand brushed Sara's fingers. Their eyes locked. The glass slipped from her grasp and crashed to the floor. Sara swept past me as she ran into the villa.

I left Asad to his friends, who had become impatient and begun to empty into the garden. They were more flustered by the sight of my face than of my huge protruding belly. I defiantly waddled by them, and made a point of greeting them full in the face. They responded with embarrassed mumbles.

Kareem awoke me at midnight. When he arrived at the palace, he had been intercepted by Asad. Kareem wanted to know from me what had happened in the garden. I sleepily related the evening's occurrence and enquired about Asad's health.

I sat up with a start when Kareem replied that Asad was insisting on marrying Sara. He had announced to Kareem that he would never know happiness if Sara were not his wife. This, from the playboy of all playboys! A man who had, only a few short weeks earlier, saddened his mother when he vehemently swore never to marry.

I was astonished. I told Kareem that it was easy to surmise Asad's attraction to Sara by his behaviour in the garden, but that this insistence on marriage was unbelievable! After a few moments of visual pleasure? I dismissed it as nonsense and turned back on my side.

While Kareem was showering, I rethought the event and left our bed. I knocked on Sara's door. Since there was no answer, I slowly pushed the door open. My sister was sitting on the balcony staring at a star-filled sky.

With great difficulty, I manoeuvred myself into a corner of the balcony and sat, silent, in a stupor at this turn of events.

Without looking in my direction, Sara spoke with certainty. 'He wishes to marry me.'

'Yes,' I agreed in a small voice.

With a burning look in her eyes Sara continued. 'Sultana, I saw my life ahead of me when I looked into his soul. This is the man Huda saw when she said I would know love. She also said that as a result of this love I would bring six little ones into the world.'

I closed my eyes in an attempt to bring to mind the comments made by Huda on that day long ago in our parents' home. I remembered talk of Sara's unrealized ambitions and the mention of marriage, but little else of the conversation remained fresh in my mind. I shivered when I realized that much of what Huda had predicted had come true.

I felt compelled to dismiss the idea of love at first sight. But I suddenly recalled my charged emotions the day I first met Kareem. I bit my tongue and made no sound.

Sara patted my belly. 'Go to bed, Sultana. Your child needs rest. My destiny will come to me.' She turned her gaze back to the stars. 'Tell Kareem that Asad should go and speak with Father of this matter.'

When I returned to the bed, Kareem was awake. I repeated Sara's words, and he shook his head in wonder and muttered that life was indeed strange, then wrapped his arms around my belly. Sleep came easily to us, for our lives were fixed on a carefully charted course, and neither of us expected unknowns.

The following morning I left Kareem to his shaving and moved heavily down the staircase. I heard Noorah before I saw her. She, as was her favourite pastime, was quoting a proverb. I cursed under my breath but listened quietly at the doorway.

' "The man who marries a woman for her beauty will be deceived; he who marries a woman for good sense can truly say he is married." '

I had no feeling left to fight so I thought to cough to announce my presence. When Noorah began to speak again I changed my mind. I held my breath and strained my ears to hear her words.

'Asad, the girl has been married before. She was quickly divorced. Who knows the reason? Reconsider, my son. You can wed whom you wish. You will be wise to start with a woman that is fresh, not one that is wilted from use! Besides, my son, you see the ball of fire that is Sultana. Can her sister be of a different substance?'

I followed my stomach into the room, my heart aflutter. She was cautioning Asad against Sara. Not only that; the leopard had not changed its spots: in secret Noorah still hated me. I was a bitter potion for her to swallow.

Aware of Asad's carefree character, I had not been in favour of his and Sara's love. Now I would be a resolute supporter of their wishes. Relieved, I could easily see by Asad's expression that nothing would alter his plans. He was a man possessed.

The conversation folded when they saw my face, for I have difficulty in clothing anger; I was furious that Noorah assumed that grief would arise from her son's union with my sister. Surely, I could not argue against my own rebellious nature. I had assumed the role at an early age and had no inclination to alter. But for Sara to be labelled with my reputation was maddening!

In my youth, I had heard many old women say: 'If you stand near a blacksmith you will get covered in soot; but if you stand near a perfume-seller you will carry an aroma of scent with you.' I realized that, as far as Noorah was concerned, Sara was carrying the soot of her younger sister. My feeling was now bottomless rage at my mother-in-law.

Sara's beauty had sparked jealousy in many of our sex. I knew that her appearance closed the possibility of any consideration given to her gentle character and blazing intellect. Poor Sara!

Asad stood up and nodded slightly in my direction. He excused himself from our company. Noorah looked like someone suffering from a dagger wound when he turned back to her and said: 'The decision is made. If I am acceptable to her and her family, no-one can delay me.'

Noorah yelled at his back about the insolence of youth and tried to load him with guilt when she exclaimed that she was not long for the world; her heart was weakening by the day. When Asad ignored her obvious ploy, she shook her head in sorrow. Brows knitted, she thoughtfully sipped at a cup of coffee. No doubt she was plotting against Sara as she had against the Lebanese woman.

In a state of high emotion, I rang the bell for the cook and ordered yoghurt and fruit for breakfast. Marci came into the room and relieved the pain of my swollen feet with her skilled fingers. Noorah attempted conversation, but I was too angry to respond. As I began to nibble fresh strawberries – flown in daily from Europe – a labour pain took me to the floor. I was frightened and screamed in agony, for this crushing pain was too soon and far too severe. I knew the pain should begin as a twinge, as the false labour that had nudged me in the past.

Chaos erupted as Noorah called out in one breath for Kareem, for Sara, for the special nurses and for the servants. In moments, Kareem lifted me in his arms and bundled me into the back of an extra-long limousine, which had been especially converted for this event. The seats had been ripped out and a bed built in on one side. Three small seats had been made ready to accommodate Kareem, Sara and a nurse. The physician from London and the other four nurses had been alerted and were following in a separate limousine.

I clutched my back while the nurse tried in vain to monitor my heartbeat. Kareem yelled at the driver to go faster; then he reversed his orders and screamed for him to go slower, declaring in a loud voice that his reckless driving would kill us all. He thumped the poor man on the back of the head when he allowed another driver to cut in front of our car.

Kareem began to curse himself for not arranging a police escort. Sara did her best to calm Kareem, but he was like an unleashed storm. Finally, the British nurse spoke loudly in his face; she advised him that his conduct was harmful to his wife and child. She threatened to remove him from the vehicle if he did not quieten himself.

Kareem, a prominent royal prince who had known no criticism in his life from a woman, entered a state of shock and was speechless. We all breathed a sigh of relief.

The hospital administrator and a large staff that had been alerted by the household were waiting at the side-door. The administrator was delighted that our child would be born in his institution, for in those days many of the young royals travelled abroad for the event of birth.

My labour was long and difficult, for I was young and small in size and my baby was stubborn and large. I recall little of the birth itself; my mind was seduced with drugs, and my memory is hazy. The nervous tension of the staff inflated the mood of the room, and I heard the physician insult his staff time and again. Without doubt, they were, as were my husband and family, praying for the birth of a son. Their reward would be great if a male child appeared; if a female child was born, there would be great disappointment. As far as I was concerned, a female child was my desire.

My land was bound to change, and I felt myself smile with anticipation of the agreeable life my baby daughter would know.

The cheering of the physician and his staff awoke me from a shadowy hollow. A son was born! I was sure I had heard the physician whisper to his head nurse: 'The rag-head in the dress will fill my pockets for this prize!' My mind protested at this insult to my husband, but a deep slumber took me from the room and the remark was not recalled for many weeks. By that time, Kareem had awarded the physician with a new Jaguar and fifty thousand English pounds. His nurses were presented with gold jewellery from the *souq* along with five thousand English pounds each. The jubilant hospital administrator from Egypt received a substantial contribution to be used for the maternity wing. He was overjoyed with a bonus of three months' salary.

All thoughts of a daughter vanished when my yawning son was placed in my arms. A daughter would come later. This male child would be taught different and better ways than the generation before him. I felt the power of my intentions creating his future. He would not be backward in his thinking; his sisters would be given a place of honour and respect; and he would know and love his partner before he wed. The vast possibilities of his accomplishments glowed and glittered as a new star. I told myself that many times in history one man has created change that influenced millions. I swelled with pride as I considered the good to mankind that would flow from the tiny body in my arms. Without doubt, the new beginning of women in Arabia could start with my own blood.

Kareem gave little thought to the future of his son. He was enamoured of fatherhood and quite rash with foolish statements regarding the number of sons we would produce together.

We were mindless with joy!

Chapter Fifteen

Dark Secrets

The completion of our birth is in death. Life begins with only one passageway; however, there are unlimited means of exit. The usual and hoped-for method of departure follows the wondrous fulfilment of life's promise. When death claims one blooming with life and cause for hope, it is the saddest of all events. When blossoming youth ends as the result of another man's hand, it is the worst of life.

At the rapturous occasion of the birth of my son, I was confronted with the mindless death of a young and innocent girl.

Kareem and the medical staff attempted to cloister me from the other Saudi women who were short steps away from my suite. While my son slept beside me with an entourage for protection, other sons and daughters were kept in the nursery. Curiosity about their life-stories lured me from my rooms. As with most of the royals, I had led a life sheltered from ordinary citizens, and now my inquisitive nature led me to conversation with these women.

If my childhood had been bleak, the lives of most Saudi women had been more bleak, I soon learned.

My life was ruled by men, but there was protection of sorts because of my family name. The majority of women gathered around the nursery window had no voice in their destiny.

I was eighteen years old at the time of my first child's birth. I met girls as young as thirteen nursing their young. Other young women no more than my own age were delivering their fourth or fifth infant.

One young girl intrigued me. Her black eyes were dulled with pain as she gazed at the mass of screaming infants. She stood so quietly for such a lengthy time that I knew her eyes did not see what was before her; instead she was immersed in a drama far from the spot on which we were standing.

I learned that she was from a small village, not distant from the city. Normally, women in her tribe gave birth in their homes, but she had been in labour five long days and nights, and her husband had driven her to the city for medical assistance. I befriended her over a period of several mornings and discovered that she had been married at the age of twelve to a man of fifty-three. She was the third wife, but much favoured by her husband.

Muhammad, our beloved Prophet of Islam, taught that men should divide their time equally among their wives. In this case, the husband was so occupied with the charms of his young bride that, to please their husband, wives numbers one and two frequently sanctioned their approval of losing their turns for mating. The young girl said her husband was a man of great power and did 'it' many times a day. Her eyes widened as she moved her arm up and down in the pumping motion for added effect.

Now she was frightened, for she had given birth to a daughter, not a son. Her husband would be angry when he came to claim them for the trip back to the village, for the firstborn of the other two wives had been sons. Now, with foreboding, she sensed that she would be scorned by her husband.

She recalled little of her childhood, which now seemed ages ago. She had been raised poorly, and experienced little but hard work and sacrifice. She described how she had helped her numerous brothers and sisters to herd the goats and camels and tend to a small garden. I was anxious to know her feelings of men and women and life, but since she was sadly lacking in education I did not receive the answers I was seeking.

She was gone before I could say goodbye. I felt cold from the thought of her bleak life and wandered back to my suite in a despondent state.

In a fit of anxiety over the safety of his son, Kareem had posted armed guards at the door of my suite. When I had made my morning walk to the nursery, I was surprised to see guards standing in front of another room. I thought that another princess must be in the ward. I eagerly asked a nurse to tell me the name of the princess. A crease formed on her brow when she told me that I was the only princess in the hospital.

She told me the story, but not before she had advised me that she was absolutely scandalized. Then she proceeded to insult all the people on earth before she described the happenings in room 212. She said that nothing of the sort would ever happen in her country, that the British are quite civilized, thank you, and that they make the rest of the world seem simply barbaric.

My imagination could not take me to such depths of anger, so I implored her to tell me what was happening before Kareem paid his afternoon visit.

The day before, she told me, the hospital staff had been dismayed to see a young girl about to deliver, shackled in leg-irons and handcuffs, escorted to the maternity ward by armed guards. A group of angry *mutawas*, followed by the frightened administrator, had accompanied the guards; they, not the administrator, had appointed a physician to her case.

To the physician's consternation, he had been informed that the girl had been tried in the Shari'a (the law of God) courts and found guilty of fornication. Since this was a crime of Hudud (a crime against God), the penalty was severe. The *mutawas*, clothed in self-righteousness, were there to bear witness to the appropriate punishment.

The physician, a Muslim from India, made no protest to the *mutawas*, but he was incensed at the role he was forced to play. He told the staff that the usual punishment for fornication was flogging, but in this instance the father had insisted upon death for his daughter. The girl was to be guarded until she delivered, at which time she was to be stoned to death.

The nurse's chin quivered in indignation as she reported that the girl was no more than a child. She guessed her age at fourteen or fifteen. She knew few other details and left my bedside to gossip with the other nurses in the hallway.

I begged Kareem to uncover the story. He hesitated, saying that this was not a matter of our concern. After much pleading and the shedding of tears on my part, he promised to enquire into the matter.

Sara lightened my day when she brought me bright news of her evolving romance. Asad had spoken with Father and had received the expected positive answer. Sara and Asad were going to marry within three months. I was thrilled for my sister who had known so little happiness.

Then she divulged other news that made my stomach sink with fear. She and Asad had made plans to meet in Bahrain the following weekend. When I protested, Sara said she was travelling to meet Asad, with or without my assistance. She planned to advise Father that she was still at our palace, helping me in my new role of motherhood. She would tell Noorah that she was back at Father's home. She said no-one would guess otherwise.

I asked how she could travel without Father's permission, for I knew he kept all the family passports locked in his safe at the office. Besides, she would require a letter of permission from Father or she would never gain entry to the plane. I cringed when Sara told me she had borrowed a passport and a permission letter from a girlfriend who had planned a trip to Bahrain to visit relatives but had had to cancel when one of the relatives became ill.

Since Saudi women veil, and the security guards at the airport would never dare ask to see a woman's face, many Saudi women borrow each other's passport for such occasions. The letter of permission was the added difficulty; but they, too, are swapped, along with the passports. Sara would return the good deed at a later date by planning a trip to a nearby country and cancelling at the last minute, then lending her credentials to the same friend. It was a detailed, underground operation that none of our men ever figured out. I had always been amused at the ease with which women tricked the airport officials, but now that it was my sister I was shaken with worry.

In an effort to discourage Sara from any reckless acts, I related the story of the young girl waiting to be stoned to death. Sara, as I, was distraught, but her plans remained solid. With increasing trepidation, I agreed to be her cover. She burst out laughing at the thought of meeting Asad without supervision. He had arranged to borrow a friend's apartment in Manama, the capital of the tiny country of Bahrain.

Sara, in her mood of anticipation, lifted my son from his silken cocoon. With joyful eyes, she absorbed his perfection, and said that she, too, would soon know the joys of motherhood, for she and

Asad longed for the six little ones predicted with such certainty by Huda.

I displayed the happy countenance expected by my sister but fear settled in my belly like frozen fire.

Kareem returned early in the evening with information about the condemned girl. He said she was known to be wanton and had become pregnant after having sex with numerous teenage boys. Kareem was disgusted with her behaviour. He said that in her disdain for the laws of our land she had humiliated the honour of her family name; there was no other course possible for her family to take.

I asked my husband of the punishment for the young males who had participated, but he had no answer. I suggested that they had more than likely received a stern lecture in lieu of a death sentence; in the world of Arabs, blame for unsanctioned sex is placed wholly on the shoulders of the female. Kareem stunned me with his calm acceptance of the planned execution of a child, no matter what the crime. In spite of my appeals for him to make some effort to intervene with the king, who could often attain success with a father bent on violent punishment, Kareem dismissed my cries of alarm with unconcealed irritation and insisted that the subject be dropped.

I was withdrawn and sullen when he bade me farewell. He lavished our son with kisses and promises of a perfect life while I sat dull and unresponsive.

I was preparing to depart from the hospital when the British nurse entered my suite in a white glow of anger. She brought heavy tidings of the condemned girl. She possessed an uncanny memory and recalled every painful detail, in perfect clarity, that she had been told by the physician from India. The condemned girl had given birth to a baby daughter in the early hours of the morning. Three *mutawas* had been told of the indignation from the foreign community, and they stood with the armed guards at the entry of the delivery theatre to ensure that no sympathetic foreigner assisted the girl to escape. After delivery, the girl was wheeled back into her room. The *mutawas* informed the physician that the new mother would be removed on that day and taken away to be stoned for her crime against God. The fate of the newborn had not been determined since the family had refused to raise the child as their own.

With horror in her eyes, the nurse stated that the young girl had tearfully told the physician the events that had led to her tragic situation. Her name was Amal, and she was the daughter of a shopkeeper in Riyadh. She had been only thirteen years old when the event occurred that had shattered her world. She had just begun to veil.

It was a Thursday night (equivalent to Saturday nights in the Western world). Amal's parents had travelled to the Emirates for the weekend and would not return until Saturday noon. Three Filipino house-servants were sleeping, and the driver was in his small gatehouse far removed from the main dwelling. Amal's older married siblings were living in other areas of the city. Of the family only she and her seventeen-year-old brother were left at home. Her brother and the three Filipinos had been instructed to take care of her. Her brother had taken the opportunity to entertain a large group of teenage friends while his parents were out of the country. Amal heard loud music and voices late into the evening; the games room was located directly below her bedroom. She thought that her brother and his friends were more than likely smoking marijuana, a substance with which her brother had lately become enamoured.

Finally, when the walls of Amal's bedroom began to vibrate from the sounds of the bass from the stereo, she decided to go downstairs to ask her brother and his friends to turn down their music. Dressed only in her thin nightgown, she had no intention of entering the room, just of poking her head into the doorway to yell for peace and quiet. The lights were dim, and the room was dark; her brother did not respond to her cries, so the girl went inside to look for him.

Amal's brother was not to be found. The other teenage boys in the room were obviously heated with drugs and talk of women, for Amal was pounced upon by several boys at once and found herself pinned to the floor. She screamed for her brother and tried to make the boys understand that she was the daughter of the house, but her pleas did not register in their drugged minds. Her gown was ripped from her body. She was brutally assaulted by her brother's friends, as they had turned into a frenzied mob. The volume of the music muffled the sounds of the attack, and no-one heard her screams for help. Amal lost consciousness after the third boy raped her.

Her brother had been in the bathroom, but he was so drugged that he had slumped against the wall and slept in a haze through the remainder of the night. Later, when the dawn of light cleared the heads of the attackers and Amal's true identity was revealed, the boys fled the villa.

Amal was taken to a nearby hospital by the driver and the Filipinos. The doctor in the emergency room notified the police. The *mutawas* became involved. Owing to Amal's seclusion as a female, she could not identify her attackers by name, only that they were acquaintances of her brother. Their names were taken from Amal's brother, but by the time they were collected and asked to appear before the police for statements they had taken great pains to prepare their story. According to the boys' version of the evening, no drugs had been present. They acknowledged only that they had been playing loud music and having innocent fun. They said the girl had entered the room in a sheer nightdress and enticed them to have sex. She told the boys she had been upstairs reading a book on sex and had a great deal of curiosity. They swore that they had turned her down at first, but that she had behaved in such a bold manner – sitting on their laps, kissing them and fingering her body – that they could not hold back any longer. The girl had been left without a chaperon and was determined to have a good time with some boys. They declared that she was insatiable and had begged them all to participate.

The parents returned from the Emirates. Amal's mother believed her daughter's story; although demented with grief, she was unable to convince her husband of the girl's innocence. Amal's father, who had always been uncomfortable with daughters, was stricken by the event, but felt that the boys had done only what any male would do under the circumstances. With a heavy heart, he concluded that his daughter must be punished for shaming his name. Amal's brother, fearful of severe punishment for using drugs, did not step forward to clear his sister's name.

The *mutawas* offered the father moral support in his strong stance and showered him with accolades for his religious conviction.

The girl would die today. Consumed by emotions of sorrow and fear, I barely heard the continued exclamations of the British nurse. I felt the miserable decline of my happiness as I imagined the girl's innocence and the futility of her mother's efforts to save her from a cruel death. I myself had never witnessed a stoning, but Omar had done so on three occasions and had taken great delight in describing to us the fate that awaited weak women who did not carefully guard their honour which was so prized by their men. I thought of the vivid description with which Omar had burdened my memory.

When I was twelve years of age, a woman in one of the small villages not far from Riyadh had been found guilty of adultery. She was condemned to die by stoning. Omar and our neighbours' driver decided to go and view the spectacle.

A large crowd had gathered since early morning. They were restless and waiting to see the one so wicked. Omar said that just as the crowd was becoming angry with impatience in the hot sun a young woman of about twenty-five years of age was roughly pulled out of a police car. He said she was very beautiful, just the sort of woman who would defy the laws of God.

The woman's hands were bound. Her head hung low. With an official manner, a man loudly read out her crime for the crowd to hear. A dirty rag was used to gag her mouth and a black hood was fastened around her head. She was forced to kneel. A large man, the executioner, flogged the woman upon her back fifty blows.

A truck appeared, and rocks and stones were emptied in a large pile. The man who had read off the crime informed the crowd that the execution should begin. Omar said the group of people, mostly men, rushed towards the stones and began to hurl the rocks at the woman. The guilty one quickly slumped to the ground and her body jerked in all directions. Omar said the rocks continued to thud against her body for what seemed to be an interminable time. Every so often, the stones would quieten while a doctor would check the woman's pulse. After a period of nearly two hours, the doctor finally pronounced the woman dead and the stoning ceased.

The British nurse interrupted my sad ponderings when she returned to my rooms in great agitation. The police and *mutawas* were taking the girl away for her punishment. She said that if I stood in my doorway I could see her face, for the girl was not veiled. I heard a great commotion in the hallway. Quickly, I fastened my veil around my face. My feet moved my body forward without thought or intention.

The doomed one was fragile and childlike between the tall stoic guards who led her to her fate. Her chin rested on her chest, so it was difficult to see the expression on her face. But I discerned that she was a pretty child, one who would have grown into beauty had she been allowed the opportunity to age. She glanced up with dread and peered into the sea of faces that was watching her with great curiosity. I saw that her fear was great. There were no relatives to travel with her to the grave, only strangers to see her off on the darkest of journeys.

I returned to my suite. I held my baby son with great tenderness and considered the relief I felt that he was not of the weaker sex. I gazed into his tiny face with wonder. Would he, too, uphold and thereby harden the system that was so unfair to his mother and sisters? I considered the possibility that all female babies should be put to death at birth in my land. Perhaps the stern attitude of our men would be tempered by our absence. I shuddered, and the question came into my mind.

How could a mother protect the young of her own sex from the laws of the land?

The eyes of the stalwart British nurse were wet with tears. She sniffled and asked why I, a princess, did not intervene in such madness. I told her that I could not help the one condemned; women are not allowed a voice in my land, not even women of the royal family. With sorrow I told the nurse that not only would the girl die as scheduled, but also her death would be hard and her life and death would go unrecorded. With bitterness, I thought of the truly guilty ones roaming free, without thought or care for the tragic death they had wrought.

Kareem arrived with a joyful face. He had organized our return to the palace as carefully as a plan of campaign. Police escorts eased our journey through the bustling traffic of the growing city of Riyadh. Kareem told me to hush when I related the incident at the hospital. He had no desire to hear such sadness with his new son in his arms, travelling towards his destiny as a prince in a land that soothed and nurtured such a one as he.

My feelings for my husband suffered as I saw that he cared little for the fate of a lowly girl. I gave a deep sigh and felt lonely and afraid of what I and my future daughters might face in the years to come.

Chapter Sixteen

Death of a King

The year 1975 holds bittersweet memories for me; it was a year of both glittering happiness and discouraging sadness for my family and my country.

Surrounded by those who loved him, Abdullah, my adored son, celebrated his second birthday. A small circus from France was brought over on our private planes to entertain. The circus stayed for a week at the palace of Kareem's father.

Sara and Asad had survived their daring courtship and were now happily married and awaiting their first child. Asad, in great expectation of the child to be born, had flown to Paris and purchased all the baby clothes in stock at three large stores. Noorah, his disbelieving mother, told all who would listen that Asad had lost his mind. Enveloped in such love, my long-suffering sister Sara beamed with happiness at last.

Ali was studying in the United States and was no longer intimately involved in his sisters' affairs. He gave Father the fright of his life when he announced that he was in love with an American working-class woman but, much to Father's relief, Ali was fickle and soon informed us that he preferred to have a Saudi wife. We later discovered that the woman had struck Ali over the head with a candlestick when he became belligerent and demanding at her refusal to be obedient.

We young modern-thinking Saudi couples embraced the subtle relaxation of the severe restrictions upon women as the years of efforts by King Faisal and his wife Iffat for women's education and freedom proved successful. Along with our education came a determination to change our country. A few women no longer covered their faces, discarding their veils and bravely staring down the religious men who dared to challenge them. They still covered their hair and wore *abaayas*, but the bravery of these few gave hope to us all. We royals would never be allowed such freedom; it was the middle class that showed their strength. Schools for women were now opening without public demonstrations of disapproval by the *mutawas*. We felt certain that women's education would eventually lead to our equality. Unfortunately, the punishment of death for women among the uneducated fundamentalists still occurred. One small step at a time, we grimly reminded each other.

Suddenly, over a six-month period, Kareem and I became the owners of four new homes. Our new palace in Riyadh was finally completed. Kareem decided his new son would grow more hardy if he inhaled fresh sea breezes, so we purchased a new villa by the seaside in Jeddah. My father owned a spacious apartment-house in London only four streets away from Harrods, and he offered the property, at a grand bargain, to any of his children who might be interested. Since my other sisters and their husbands already owned apartments in London, and Sara and Asad were in the process of purchasing an apartment in Venice, Kareem and I eagerly seized the opportunity to have a home in that colourful city so loved by Arabs. And finally, as a special three-year wedding anniversary gift for presenting him with a precious son, Kareem bought me a lovely villa in Cairo.

Upon the occasion of Abdullah's birth, the family jeweller had flown to Riyadh from Paris to bring a selection of diamonds, rubies and emeralds that he had designed into seven distinctive necklace, bracelet and earring sets. Needless to say, I felt richly rewarded for doing what I had wanted to do.

Kareem and I spent as much time as possible in Jeddah. Happily, our villa was located in a coveted spot frequented by the royal family.

We played backgammon as we watched our son, surrounded by Filipino maids, paddle in the warm blue waters that teemed with exotic fish. Even we females were allowed to swim, though we kept our *abaayas* tight around us until we were up to our necks in water. One of the servants relieved me from the *abaaya* held high with my hand, so that I could swim and splash with abandon. I was as free as it was possible for a woman to be in Saudi Arabia.

It was the end of March, not a hot month of the year, so we did not linger long after the midday sun. I told the servants to gather our laughing baby and rinse him under the specially made portable hot shower. We watched him as he gurgled and kicked his short fat legs. Our smiles were broad with pride; Kareem squeezed my hand and said he felt guilty for feeling such happiness. I accused him later of bringing us, and all Saudis, bad luck by voicing his joy with life.

Most Arabs believe in the evil eye; never do we speak aloud of our joy with life or of the beauty of our children. Quite possibly, some evil spirit will hear and steal the object of our joy or cause us some grief by taking away a loved one. To ward off this evil eye, our babies are protected by blue beads pinned to their clothing. As enlightened as we were, our son was no exception.

Moments later, we recoiled in horror as Asad ran towards us with the words 'King Faisal is dead! Murdered by one of the family!' Struck dumb, we sat quivering as Asad told us the scanty details he had learned from a royal cousin.

At the root of our uncle's death was a dispute about the opening of a television station that had occurred nearly ten years before. King Faisal had always stood firm for the progress of modernization for our backward land. Kareem said he had heard him say once that, whether we Saudis liked it or not, he was going to pull us, kicking and screaming, into the twentieth century.

The problems he faced with the extremely religious citizens were a continuation of vexing situations encountered by our very first ruler and Faisal's father, Abdul Aziz. These men of religion fought furiously against the opening of the first radio station, and our first king overcame the objections by ordering the Koran read over the airwaves. The religious ones could find little fault in such a speedy method of spreading God's word. Years later, when Faisal strove to provide television stations for our people, he, like his father before him, encountered much opposition from the Ulema (the religious sheikhs).

Tragically, members of the royal family joined in such protests, and in September 1965, when I was but a child, one of our cousins was shot and killed by the police as he led a demonstration against a television station a few miles outside Riyadh. The renegade prince, with his followers in tow, had stormed the station. This episode ended in a rifle battle with the police, and he was killed. Nearly ten years had passed, but hate had bubbled in the younger brother of the prince until he had now retaliated by shooting and killing his uncle, the king.

Kareem and Asad flew to Riyadh. Sara and I, along with various female royal cousins, congregated within the confines of a family walled palace. We all wailed and shouted our grief to each other. There were few female cousins who did not love King Faisal, for he was our sole chance for change and ultimate freedom. He alone had the prestige with both the religious men and the royal factions of our land to further the cause of women. He felt our chains as his own, and beseeched our fathers to stand behind him in his quest for social change. Once I myself heard him say that even though there are separate roles for men and women, as directed by God, no sex should rule with unquestioned supremacy over the other. With a quiet voice he said that he would know little happiness until each citizen of his land, both male and female, was the master of his or her own fate. He believed that only through the education of our women would our cause be enforced, for our ignorance has surely kept us in darkness. Certainly, no ruler since Faisal has championed our plight. Looking back, our short but heady climb to freedom began its slippery descent the moment his life exploded with the bullets of deceit from his own family. Sadly, we women knew that our one chance for freedom was buried with King Faisal.

Each of us felt anger and hatred for the family that had bred such a one as our cousin, Faisal ibn Musaid, the slayer of our hopes and dreams. One of my cousins shouted out that the slayer's father himself was not right in his mind. He, who had been born prominent in the scheme of Saudi royalty, a half-brother of King Faisal himself, had shunned all contact with family members and responsibility of the throne. One son had been a fanatic, willing to die to prevent the innocent installation of a television station, and another son had killed our beloved and respected King Faisal.

No pain could be worse than the thought of Saudi Arabia without such wisdom to guide us. Never before or since have I witnessed such national grief. It was as if our entire land and all its people were swathed in agony. The best leadership our family had to offer had been struck down by one of our own.

Three days later, Sara's daughter surprised her mother by entering the world as a breach baby. Little Fadeela, named for our mother, joined a nation in mourning. Our grief was so deep that recovery was sluggish, but little Fadeela revived our minds and we recalled the message of joy through her new life.

Sara, in her fear for her daughter's future, convinced Asad to sign a document that said their daughter would be free to choose her husband without family interference. Sara had suffered a troubling nightmare that she and Asad were killed in a plane crash and her daughter was raised in the rigid manner of our generation. Sara, staring pointedly at Asad, said she would commit murder rather than see her daughter wed to a man of evil schemes. Asad, still wild with love for his wife, comforted her by signing the paper and by establishing a Swiss bank account in the baby's name for a million dollars. Sara's daughter would have the legal and financial means to escape her personal nightmares should necessity arise.

Ali returned from the United States for the summer holiday and, if it were possible, he was even more obnoxious than I recalled. He made a great point of telling us of his escapades with American women and announced that, yes, it was true, just as he had been told, they were all whores!

When Kareem interrupted and stated that he had met many women of high morals when he was in

Washington, Ali laughed and suggested that much had changed. He declared that the women he had met in bars took the initiative and proposed sex before he had had the opportunity even to bring up the subject. Kareem told him that was the issue; if a woman were alone in a bar, she was more than likely looking for a one-night stand or a good time. After all, women were free in America, the same as men. He advised Ali to attend church or cultural events, where he would be surprised at the conduct of the women. Ali was adamant. He said that he had tested the morals of women from all walks of life in America; they were *all* definitely whores, in his experience.

Like most Muslims, Ali would never see or understand the customs and traditions of another religion or land. The only knowledge most Arabs have of American society comes from the content of low-grade American movies and trashy television shows. Most important, Saudi men travel alone. Because of their forced seclusion from female companionship, their only interest lies in foreign women. Sadly, they seek out only women who work in bars as strippers or prostitutes. This slanted view distorts Saudis' opinions of the morality of the West. Since most Saudi women do not travel, they believe the stories told by their husbands and brothers. As a result, the vast majority of Arabs truly believe that most Western women are promiscuous.

Admittedly, my brother was handsome in an exotic way that would attract many of the opposite sex, but I knew without a doubt that every woman in America was not a whore! I told Kareem that I longed for the opportunity to travel with Ali. What fun it would be to stand behind him and hold up a sign that proclaimed: THIS MAN SECRETLY DISDAINS YOU AND HOLDS YOU IN CONTEMPT! IF YOU SAY YES TO THIS MAN, HE WILL BRAND YOU A WHORE TO THE WORLD!

Before Ali left to return to the States, he told Father he was ready to acquire his first wife. Life without sex was a hardship, he said, and he would like a woman to be available to him each time he returned to Riyadh for the holidays. Most important, it was time for him, Ali, to have a son. For without sons a man has no value in Saudi Arabia, and is scorned by all who know him.

His new wife could not live with him in the United States, of course; but, rather, would live in Father's villa, carefully guarded by Omar and the other servants. Ali said he must be free to enjoy the relaxed morals of America. His only requirement for his wife – other than virginity, of course – was that she be young, no more than seventeen years of age, exceptionally beautiful, and obedient. Within two weeks, Ali was engaged to a royal cousin; a wedding date was set for December, when he would have more than a month between school terms.

Observing my brother, I recognized my good fortune in having wed a man like Kareem. Doubt-less my husband was far removed from perfection, but Ali was a typical Saudi male; to have such a one as him as your master would make life a grinding affair.

Prior to Ali's return to the States, our family gathered at our villa in Jeddah. One evening, the men had too much to drink and became argumentative. After dinner, the volatile issue of whether women should drive cars came out into the open for debate. Kareem and Asad joined Sara and me in our push for a change in the silly custom that had no basis whatsoever in Islam. We brought up the example of women piloting planes in industrialized nations while we were not allowed to drive a car! Many Saudi families could not afford more than one driver, and where did that leave the family when he was on an errand? What would happen if a medical emergency occurred when the driver was unavailable? Did Saudi men think so little of their women's abilities that they would rather twelve- and thirteen-year-old boys drive (which is common in Saudi Arabia) than adult women?

Ali, Father and Ahmed thought the very topic maddening. Ali declared that women and men would be meeting in the deserts for sexual misadventures! Ahmed worried about the veil's hindrance to visibility. Father brought up the possibility of car accidents, and the vulnerability of the female on the street while awaiting the traffic officer. Father looked around the room for confirmation from his other sons-in-law that a woman behind the wheel of a car would endanger herself and others in the process. My other sisters' husbands busied themselves refreshing their drinks or going to the bathroom.

Finally, with brash confidence, as if he had the one bright idea that would win the argument, Ali said that since women are more easily influenced than men they would imitate the youth of our land, who raced their cars through the streets. Naturally, the women would have no thoughts except to emulate them, and this would, as a result, cause our already soaring accident rate to climb.

My brother still infuriated me! Ali mistakenly believed that I had left my youthful impulses behind, but his smug look gave rise to my temper. To everyone's complete surprise, I leaped at Ali, grabbed a handful of his hair, and began to pull as hard as I could. It took both Kareem and Father to force me to release my grasp. My sisters' loud laughter rang throughout the room while their husbands stared at me with a combination of awe and fear.

Ali tried to make peace with me the following day before he departed for the States. My hate was so reckless that I purposely manoeuvred him into a conversation about marriage and the insistence of our men that their wives be virgins while they themselves tried to sample as many women as possible. Ali took the conversation seriously and proceeded to quote the Koran and enlighten me on the absolute necessity of the virginity of females.

The old Sultana of many sly tricks came back to me with ease. I shook my head sadly and sighed a deep sigh. Ali asked what was in my heart. I told him that for once he had convinced me. I agreed with him that all females should be virgins when they wed. I added, with a hidden malice he did not see, that the nature of our young girls had so changed that rarely was a real virgin to be found among them. At Ali's questioning look, I said that certainly there was little misconduct from Saudi women while in Arabia, for what woman wants to lose her life? But when our females travelled, I asserted, they sought out sexual partners and gave their most precious gift to strangers.

Ali became enraged at the thought of any man other than himself, a Saudi, deflowering a Saudi virgin! He enquired, with great agitation, as to where I had learned such information. With a look of appeal on my face, I begged my brother not to reveal our conversation, for surely Father and Kareem would be scandalized. But I admitted to him that we women discussed such issues, and that it was a known topic: the day of the virgin was leaving our land!

Ali puckered his lips and sank deep in thought. He asked me what these young girls did on their wedding night; for if there was no blood, a girl would be disgraced and returned to her father. In Arabia, bloodied sheets are still proudly handed to the mother-in-law of the bride so that she can show friends and relatives that a woman of honour and purity has joined her family.

I leaned closer and told Ali that most young women had surgery to repair their hymen. I added that most young women gave their virginity over and over again to unsuspecting males. It was simple and easy to fool a man. There were plenty of physicians who skilfully performed the operation in Europe, and a few who were known for the service in Saudi Arabia.

Then, to Ali's total horror, I whispered that if, by some chance, the girl could not have a repair job in time for her marriage it was a simple affair to place the liver of a sheep inside her prior to the sex act. The husband could not tell the difference. It was a sheep liver he was deflowering, and not his wife!

A new fear engrossed my self-centred brother. He immediately placed an urgent call to a physician friend; holding the telephone, his face became pale when the friend admitted that such operations were possible. As for the sheep liver, the physician had not heard of it, but it sounded like a viable scheme immoral women would discover sooner or later.

Obviously disturbed, Ali returned twice to the villa on that day, asking my advice as to how he could best guard against such trickery. I told him there was no way, unless he had kept company with his new bride day and night since the day she was born. He, Ali, would just have to accept the possibility that the one he wed might very well be human and have committed mistakes in her youth.

A worried and despondent Ali returned to the States.

When I told Kareem, Sara and Asad of my joke, Sara could not control her glee. Kareem and Asad exchanged looks of worry and glanced at their wives with new thoughts.

Ali's wedding remained on schedule. His young bride was achingly beautiful. How I pitied her. But Sara and I laughed aloud when we saw that Ali was frantic with worry. Later my husband reprimanded me for my mischief when Ali confessed to him that he, Ali, was now dreading the act of sex. What if he had been tricked? He would never know and would be forced to live in doubt with this wife and all future wives.

The worst possible nightmare for a Saudi male would be to follow another in an act of sex with the woman he had wed. If the woman were a prostitute, there was no shame, but his wife represented his family name, bore his sons. The very thought that he might have been misled was more than my brother could bear.

I readily admitted to my husband that I had wicked moments and acknowledged without hesitation that I would have to face up to many sins on my day of judgement. Yet, on Ali's wedding night, I smiled with a satisfaction I had never known. I had discovered and exploited Ali's greatest fear.

Chapter Seventeen

The Woman's Room

Nura's hand was shaking as she retrieved the Koran, our holy book. She pointed out a section to me. I looked at Nura and then, one by one, at my other sisters. My gaze rested on Tahani's stricken face. All hope was lost for her friend Sameera.

Sara, usually quiet and restrained, now spoke. 'No-one can help her. The Prophet, himself, ordered this method of punishment.'

Anger flamed out of my body as I retorted: 'Sameera was not guilty of lewdness. She merely fell in love with a Westerner! These men of ours have determined it is permissible for them to mate with a foreign woman, a woman of another religion, but no, we women are forbidden! It is insane! This law – and its interpretation – is made by men, for men!'

Nura tried to calm me, but I was prepared to fight to the last desperate inch this unnatural tyranny now focused on one whom we all loved: Sameera.

The day before, Sameera had been sentenced by the men of her family and of her religion to be confined to a room of darkness until she was claimed by death. Sameera was twenty-two. Death would come slowly to one so young and strong of limb.

Her crime? While in school in London, she had met and fallen in love with one not of our faith. From our first age of understanding, we Saudi women are taught that it is a sin for any Muslim woman to bind herself to a non-Muslim: the religion of her children cannot be guaranteed if her husband is Christian or Jewish. Since the last word in the Middle Eastern family rests with the husband, the children might well be brought up as Christian or Jewish; the wife and mother would have no say.

Every Muslim is taught that Islam is the final message from Allah to mankind and, therefore, it is the faith superior to all others. Muslims are not allowed to bring themselves knowingly under the patronage of non-Muslims, nor should they ever allow such a relationship to develop. Yet many Saudi *men* do marry women of other faiths without repercussions. Only Saudi *women* pay the supreme price for their association with a non-believer. Our religious scholars say the union of Muslim men with women of other faiths is permissible, for the children are raised in the superior Muslim faith of their father.

Just thinking about the unfairness of it all made me scream out in rage. My sisters and I understood that from this moment the stepping-stones of Sameera's life, one by one, would lead to a great tragedy. And we, her friends from childhood, were helpless in our desire to rescue her.

Sameera had been Tahani's dearest friend since

the age of eight. She was an only child; her mother had fallen ill with ovarian cancer and, although cured, she was told there would be no other children. Surprisingly, Sameera's father had not divorced his now barren wife, which would have been customary for the majority of Saudi men.

My sisters and I had all known women stricken with serious illnesses, only to be thrust aside by their husbands. The social stigma of divorce is severe, and the financial and emotional trauma overwhelming for women. If the children of a divorced woman are not suckling, they, too, can be taken from her. If divorced women are fortunate, they will have loving parents to welcome them home, or an elder son who will give them shelter. Without a supportive family, they are doomed, for no single or divorced woman can live alone in my land. There are government-sponsored homes built specifically to accommodate such women, but life is bleak and each moment is cruel. Those few divorced women who have an opportunity to re-marry are lucky enough either to be a great beauty or to have a great fortune. As with everything else in Saudi society, the failure of the marriage and the blame for divorce rest with the woman.

Sameera's mother had been one of the fortunate. Her husband loved her truly and did not think of casting her aside at her time of greatest need. He did not even take a second wife to provide him with sons. Sameera's father is a man considered strange in our society.

Sameera and Tahani were the best of friends.

And, since Sara and I were closest to Tahani in age, we were playmates of Sameera, too. All three of us were envious of Sameera in many ways, for her father bestowed great passion on his only child. He, unlike most Saudi men of his generation, was of a modern mind and promised his daughter that she would be free of the antiquated customs forced upon the females of our land.

Sameera had felt our pain at the obvious failings in our father. In every crisis she had stood firm with the passion of our cause. My eyes stung as I recalled Sameera's tears at Sara's wedding. She had clung to my neck, moaning that Sara would die in the harness of servitude! And now she, Sameera, was locked in the darkest of prisons where even servants were forbidden to speak as they pushed her meals through a special slot at the base of the only door. She was never to hear another human voice. Her total world would be only the sound of her own breathing.

The thought was unbearable. I turned to Sara and suggested that Kareem and Asad might lend some assistance. Tahani looked up in expectation. Sara shook her head slowly. Asad had already made enquiries; neither the uncle nor Sameera's former husband would lift the harsh sentence of darkness with silence until death. This was a matter between the family and their God.

The year of my wedding, Sameera had already charted her future with great care. Since an early age, she had had the odd idea to become an engineer. No woman in Saudi Arabia had such a degree, for we are directed to careers considered appropriate for females: paediatricians, teachers, or social workers for women and children.

In addition, Saudi female students are forbidden contact with male teachers, so Sameera's father had hired his daughter a tutor from London. After years of concentration and effort studying at home, Sameera had been accepted by a technical school in London. Her father, in great pride of his beautiful and clever child, accompanied his wife and daughter to London.

Sameera's father and mother settled Sameera in a private dwelling. Two Indian female servants and an Egyptian secretary were employed to live with their daughter. They bade their child farewell and returned to Riyadh. Of course, no-one had a thought that they would never see each other again. The months passed and, as we expected, Sameera excelled in school.

During her fourth month in London, Sameera met Larry, an exchange student from California. Opposites attract, as they say, for Larry was tall, muscular and blond, a California free spirit, while Sameera was exotic, slim, and mired in the confusions created by our oppressive men.

She wrote to Tahani that love had made her heart heavy, for she knew she was forbidden to marry a Christian. Larry was a Catholic who would never agree to convert to the Muslim faith, a procedure that would help their situation.

Within the month, Tahani received a second, more desperate letter; Sameera and Larry could not survive apart. She was going to live with him while in London, and later she would escape to the States where they would marry. Then, Sameera said, her parents could purchase a home near their daughter in the States. She was certain that their close family relationship would not suffer. But she would be forced to forfeit her Saudi nationality. We would never see her again in our country, for she understood that she could not return to our land after such a scandalous event as marriage to a non-believer.

Tragically, Sameera's parents never learned of their daughter's dilemma, for both of them and their driver were killed instantly when a water-tanker crashed into the side of their car as it crossed a busy street in Riyadh.

In the Arab world, when the head of the family (always a male) dies, the eldest brother takes control of the affairs of the surviving family members. Upon Sameera's father's death, his eldest brother was now her guardian.

Never have two men of the same family borne so little resemblance to each other. Where Sameera's father was permissive and loving, his brother was stern and unbending. A man of the deepest faith, he had often expressed his profound displeasure at the independence of his brother's daughter.

Scandalized, he had not spoken to Sameera's father since the day Sameera enrolled in the school in London. Scornful of the education of girls, he thought it best that females be married at a tender age to a man of years and wisdom. He had recently wed a thirteen-year-old child. She had begun her menses a few months back and was the daughter of a man such as himself.

Sameera's uncle was the father of four daughters and three sons; his daughters had been safely wed at the first sign of puberty. They received little schooling other than the female arts of cooking and sewing, although they had ample instruction in reading skills so that they could recite the Koran.

The day following her parents' death, Sameera received a second shock. A communication of command arrived from her uncle, who was now the head of her family: 'Return to Riyadh on the earliest flight. Bring all that belongs to you.'

Her fear of the brutal realism of life under the care of her uncle caused Sameera to gather her courage and plunge irrationally into a headlong course of unknowns. In what proved to be a fatal mistake for her, Sameera and Larry fled together to California.

The blatant disobedience of this female child burned into the heart of Sameera's new guardian. At that time, he had no knowledge of Sameera's foreign lover. He had no understanding of the wayward girl, for he had no experience with unyielding females.

By the end of the month, with no information of Sameera's whereabouts, the uncle imagined his niece dead, her body decaying in a heathen land. His hunt for her intensified without results, until finally, at the insistence of his eldest son, he relented and employed the services of a detective agency to trace the path of his brother's only child.

Early one morning, Sameera's tyrannical uncle, roaring with rage, arrived at Tahani's villa, clutching the agency's report. He demanded that my sister, Sameera's confidante, reveal the location of his 'ungodly niece and her infidel lover'.

Eyes wide as she described the scene, Tahani marvelled at his anger. He banged his head against the walls of her home; he cried to Allah for assistance in slaying his niece; with fierce denunciations, he promised revenge upon the heathen lover. He cursed the day his brother's child was born. He prayed aloud for God to heap calamities upon his faithless niece. He declared that she had ruined the honour of the family for generations to come.

Tahani, overwhelmed by his shouting and violence, fled from her home to the offices of her husband, Habbib. When they returned to their palace, Sameera's uncle had since departed, but not without a dire warning to the servants that the one who sheltered his niece would feel his wrath. To soothe Tahani's fears, Habbib sought out the uncle and calmed his angry malice. He assured him that his niece was not in contact with our family.

Isolated as she was in another country, Sameera was unaware that her uncle, in a ceaseless effort to locate his niece, now confiscated all family members' mail. By promising great punishment should any contact with his niece escape his attention, he intimidated the family. The girl would eventually long for contact with those of her blood; when the 'one of great sin', as he deemed Sameera, weakened, she would not slip past his vigilant eye. He needed only to wait.

Meanwhile, in California, Larry grew uncertain of his love, and Sameera thrashed about as one lost. Her lover's new indifference bit deeply into her heart; she called Tahani in great fear and uncertainty as to her future course. What should she do? She had few funds and fewer friends in her new land. Without marriage to Larry, she would not be allowed to remain in America. Habbib, while allowing Tahani the freedom of her friendship with Sameera, refused his wife's request to send money.

With only a few thousand dollars left in her bank account, Sameera, in an act of desperation, called her dearest aunty, the youngest sister of her father. The aunty, in dread of her brother's power, dutifully reported the call of her niece. Notified of his niece's difficulties, the uncle carefully planned for her capture and return to his influence.

Sameera was lured to Cairo with the promise of peaceful re-entry into the family she had fled. Money was sent for her return trip. Sameera telephoned Tahani and tearfully confided that she had little choice. Larry's love had dissolved, and he had no inclination to assist her financially. She had not yet earned her degree and could not earn a salary. She had no money. She had placed telephone calls to the Saudi embassies in Washington and London. The embassy staff were unsympathetic. After she had explained her situation, she was curtly told she would have to return to her family. Escape from reality was impossible; she must return to Saudi Arabia.

Sameera told Tahani she was fearfully hopeful that her aunties were speaking the truth, for they had given their oath that their brother had softened and had agreed for her to continue her educational courses in London. Perhaps, after all, her uncle would treat the only child of his brother with kindness. Tahani, certain that the wrath of the uncle had not diminished, was unable to voice her caution, for she saw clearly the futility of Sameera's position.

Sameera was met at Cairo airport by two aunties and two male cousins. They quietened her apprehensions with talk of her return to London, once she had repaired her isolation from her family. Happily, Sameera concluded that all would be well.

Sameera returned to Riyadh.

When Sameera's expected telephone call did not come, Tahani fell into the deepest depression. She finally called Sameera's relatives, only to be informed that the child had a small fever and did not feel well enough to speak to her friends. Tahani was assured that Sameera would contact her the moment her health improved.

The second week of her return, one of Sameera's aunties answered Tahani's plea with the news that a marriage had been arranged, and that Sameera wished for Tahani to cease her contacts, for her future husband did not look favourably upon his wife's girlhood friends.

Sameera finally managed to contact Tahani. Her hopes had been dashed from the moment she saw her uncle, she said. He had been waiting for their meeting, his fury building, until it had peaked at the sight of his 'Godless' niece.

Since the night of her return, Sameera had been confined to her room, awaiting the verdict of her uncle. No member of her family dared raise a voice of protest at her mistreatment. She whispered to Tahani that she had been informed that a suitable marriage had been arranged; she would be wed within the month. Sameera was terrified at the thought, for her relationship with Larry had been one of deep love; she was no longer a virgin.

We were able to discover few details of the wedding, for no-one outside Sameera's family was invited. We knew for certain that it was not a union of joy. We learned that the groom was in his mid-fifties and that Sameera was the third wife.

Much later, Habbib was enlightened of the family gossip by one of Sameera's male cousins. He said that on her wedding night Sameera had fought the husband with such strength and determination that he had barely survived the taking of what was his. The husband, we were told, was short and fat and not overly muscular. Evidently, blood had been lost, but it was that of the husband; in the fierce battle, he had had little time to verify his wife's virginity.

When Tahani questioned Sameera's aunty who now regretted her role in entrapping her niece, she was told that in the beginning the husband had been fond of the tigress he had wed. Her insults and brave defence had done little to deter his resolve to conquer her with force. But, as time passed, he wearied of Sameera's violent gestures of disdain and grew to regret the one he had taken under his roof.

Sameera had bragged to her aunty that, in her distress, she had grown bold and shouted into her husband's round face that she could not love one such as he. She, Sameera, had known the caresses of a real man, a man of strength. She scorned her husband's expertise as a lover and compared him cruelly to her tall handsome American.

Without ceremony, the husband divorced Sameera and deposited her at her uncle's door. He angrily told the uncle that the family had no honour and had knowingly wed him to one who was no longer pure. In great detail, he spoke of Sameera's 'shame' at coming to the marriage bed with memories of another in her mind.

In a bottomless black rage, the uncle sought guidance through the pages of the Koran; he soon found verses that cemented his decision to shut away the one who had shamed his family name. The former husband, still smarting from the insults on his manhood, furthered the decision by vowing to announce to all who would listen the lack of honour in the home of Sameera's uncle, unless serious punishment were meted out to the girl.

Habbib delivered the sad news to Tahani that Sameera had been sentenced to 'the woman's room', a particularly cruel punishment. A special room on the top floor of her uncle's villa had been prepared for her. A windowless padded cell had been

243

completed for the purpose of imprisoning Sameera. The windows were obstructed with cement blocks. Insulation had been installed so that the cries of the one imprisoned could not be heard. A special door had been hung, with a bottom panel adjusted to serve as an entry for food. A hole in the floor had been built for the disposal of body wastes.

Curious foreign workmen were informed that a member of the family had suffered brain injuries from an accident; it was feared that this person might harm herself or perhaps others of the family.

My sisters and I had gathered to console Tahani, who was suffering tremendous grief at the incarceration of one close to her heart. Each of us was in pain, for Sameera was one of us, a Saudi woman with no recourse against injustice.

While I plotted endless schemes of rescue, my older sisters saw the situation more clearly. They had heard stories about other such women, and knew that there was no hope of extricating Sameera from the isolation of her fading life.

For many nights sleep deserted me; I was consumed by emotions of despair and helplessness. I, too, had heard rumours of other condemned women in my country receiving the punishment of the woman's room, but I had never had a picture in my mind of the reality of the drawn and anguished howl of someone I had known, a woman who had embodied the life and hope of our land, a woman now living in utter blacknesss, without sight or sound to sustain her life.

I awoke one night thinking that I had suffered

a bad dream. I was grasping for easement when I realized that the nightmare was real; there would be no relief to those who knew Sameera and the fact that she now suffered helplessly in total captivity and isolation. The never-ending question ran through my mind: What power on earth could release her? As I stared up at the desert night sky sparkling with stars, I had to conclude there was none.

Chapter Eighteen

Second Wife

Thursday, 28 August 1980 is a day I will never forget. Kareem and I had just returned to Riyadh from Taif, a cool mountain resort. I was lounging on the sofa while one of the Filipino servants rubbed my aching feet. Our three children were at a camp in Dubai, in the Emirates, and I was bored without them.

As I looked through the stack of newspapers that had accumulated during our two months' absence, an item of interest leaped from the page of the latest newspaper. One of my relatives, the governor of Asir, Prince Khaled Al Faisal, had recently taken steps to curb the spiralling cost of marriage in his province by limiting the dowry costs that a groom had to pay to acquire a bride in his area.

The prince had placed a limit of 25,000 Saudi riyals ($7,000) as the maximum the bride's parents would be allowed to request for their daughter. The article pointed out that the directive was well received by eligible bachelors since 100,000 Saudi riyals ($27,000) was the average price of brides in the year 1980. As a result, many young men of Saudi Arabia could not afford to purchase a wife.

I read the item to the Filipino servant, but she took little note, for she had few concerns for the plight of Saudi women who were bought and sold. Mere survival was a heavy burden for most Filipinos. They thought we Saudi women were quite fortunate to have endless time on our hands and vast sums of money to spend on whatever we might fancy.

As the mother of two daughters, I did not care about the actual price of a bride, for when the occasion came for our children to wed the bridal price would be of little concern. Kareem and I were exceedingly wealthy; money failed to play a role in my daily frustrations. But I saw a trend of backward moves by the men of our family. In the confines of our homes, they spoke eloquently of freedom for women, while in legal directives they themselves wrote they kept the pressure high for the status quo and steadily pushed us back to the primitive age.

Only the total elimination of dowries would have satisfied my longing. How many years would it take before we women were no longer bought and sold as property?

I was restless and began to feel edgy, for all of my sisters, other than Sara, were still abroad. My dearest sister was in the last few weeks of her fourth pregnancy and now slept most of the daylight hours.

My life, so well planned in my youth, had not turned out as I had envisaged it. Instead, I had settled into much the same routine as my sisters and the other royal princesses I befriended.

Since the servants fed the children their morning meal and organized their days, I generally slept until noon. After a snack of fresh fruits, I would soak in the tub in a leisurely manner. After dressing, I would join Kareem or, if he were occupied, my sisters for a late lunch. We would lounge and read after our meal, and then Kareem and I would take a short nap. Afterwards, he would return to the office or visit his royal cousins while I spent a few hours with the children.

I attended women's parties in the late afternoon and returned to our palace no later than eight or nine o'clock in the evening. Kareem and I made a point of eating our evening meal with the children to learn about their activities that day. We almost always attended a dinner-party in the evenings, for we were of a most select group that entertained mixed couples. Generally, our associates were of the royal family only, but on occasion high-ranking foreigners, foreign ministers, and wealthy Saudi business families would be included in our inner circle. Since our social freedoms had not come, we of the younger generation had decided to take them by force. We knew that the religious groups seethed with anger at our mixed gatherings, yet they made no move to pressure Khalid, our revered and pious king.

For such social gatherings the women dressed with flamboyance, for we had few occasions to show off our jewels and dresses. Kareem and I were often out until two or three in the morning.

Our routine rarely wavered unless we were out of the country.

An eternal question haunted me: Was this all there was?

I could deny the facts no longer. I, the fiery Sultana, had become an ordinary, dull and listless Saudi woman, with little of real importance to occupy my days. I hated my lazy and luxurious life, but was unsure as to the steps I could take to relieve my boredom.

After the relaxing foot massage, I had an urge to walk through the gardens. In planning our own gardens, I had used Nura's lovely grounds as a reference. Nothing gave me as much peace as a stroll in the cool shade of the small forest so vigorously watered and tended by a crew of twelve men from Sri Lanka. We lived in the middle of one of the world's harshest deserts, yet our homes were surrounded by lush green gardens. Because of endless sums of money paid for plentiful water trucked in from the seaports for the four waterings each day, we wealthy Saudis could escape the stark red sands that were waiting for the slightest chance to encroach upon our cities and erase our memory from the earth. In time, the desert would win, but for now we were the masters of our land.

I stopped to rest in the gazebo specially built for Maha, our eldest daughter, who would soon celebrate her fifth birthday. She was a dreamer and spent hours upon hours hidden in the midst of the vine-covered contraption, playing complicated games with imaginary friends. She reminded me so of myself at a young age. Fortunately, she did not share the heavy revolutionary personality of her mother, for Maha enjoyed her father's love and felt no need to rebel.

I picked at the flowers overhanging Maha's favourite spot. She had left an assortment of toys in an unruly pile. I smiled and wondered how she could be so completely removed from her younger sister's character traits; for Amani, who was now three, was a child of perfection, much in the same manner as her Aunt Sara.

As I thought of my children, my depression came to me, fierce and strong. I remembered to thank God for my healthy son and two daughters, but tears welled in my eyes when I thought again about the fact that I would have no more children.

The year before, during a routine examination at the King Faisal Specialist Hospital and Research Centre here in our city, I had been diagnosed as having breast cancer. Kareem and I were shocked, for we thought of illness as belonging only to the aged. I had remained disease-free all of my life and had borne my last two children with ease. The doctors were certain I was now clean of the killer cells, but I had lost one breast. Further, I was also warned not to become pregnant.

As a precaution against desire for more little ones that would overrule common sense, Kareem and I made a decision for me to undergo sterilization. My fears had been so great that I might not live to see my three children grow that my mind was little troubled at the time by the thought of having such a small family. In Saudi Arabia, rarely does a woman stop producing children; age removes the pangs of giving birth, nothing else.

The sound of Kareem's voice interrupted my deep and troubled thoughts. I watched him as he walked briskly across the thick grass. We had suffered many arguments over the past year, for our lives were stressed by my illness. I made a sudden resolve to become the old Sultana, the girl who used to make her husband laugh with great joy and abandon. I smiled at his long athletic legs bound by the tightness of his *thobe*. The sight of him still gladdened my heart.

When he came closer I recognized that trouble was on his mind. I tossed around the possibilities, for I knew my husband's moods; it would take many moments for him to reveal his burden. I gestured with my hand for him to sit beside me. I wanted to sit as closely as our rigid customs allow, which meant our limbs could touch through our clothing so long as no-one could see.

Kareem disappointed me when he settled at the farthest corner of the gazebo. He did not return my smile of welcome. Some harm had come to the children! I jumped to my feet and asked him what bad news he brought. He seemed surprised that I anticipated unpleasant tidings. Then Kareem uttered words that I never, in my wildest expectations, thought I would hear from my husband.

'Sultana, I made a decision, a very difficult decision, some months ago. I have not discussed this matter with you owing to your illness.'

I nodded, unclear as to what was awaiting me, though I was terrified to hear his words.

'Sultana, you are, and will always be, the most important woman – wife – in my heart.'

I still had no notion of what message my husband wanted me to hear, but without doubt his words were meant to prepare me for news I would not embrace. I felt numbness creep into my face; I knew with certainty that I did not want him to reveal what change I would soon know as actuality.

'Sultana, I am a man that can afford many children. I desire ten, twenty, as many as God sees fit to give me.'

He paused for what seemed a lifetime. I held my breath in fear.

'Sultana, I am going to wed another. As the second wife, she will be there to provide children. I need nothing further from her, only children. My love is always with you.'

No sound could be heard because of the pounding in my head. I was trapped in a dark reality that I did not believe. Never, never, never had such a consideration entered the realm of possibility.

Kareem waited for my reaction. At first, I could not move. My breath finally came back to me in deep ragged gasps. The truth of his announcement slowly sank into my mind and came to life; when my strength returned, I could answer him only with a fit of passion that brought us both to the floor.

The depth of my pain could not be expressed in words. I needed to hear Kareem beg for my mercy as I clawed his face and kicked his groin and tried desperately to kill the man who was my husband.

Kareem struggled to get to his feet, but because of the sudden madness that had consumed me with violence I was possessed with great physical strength. To restrain me, Kareem had to pin me to the ground and sit astride my body.

My screams pierced the air. The names I called my husband caused the gathering servants to freeze. Like a wild creature, I spat into Kareem's face and watched his astonishment grow as he witnessed the fury he had triggered. Finally, the servants, in fear of what they were witnessing, rushed to various areas and hid themselves in buildings and behind bushes.

At last my rage was spent. A deadly calm fell over me. My mind was made up. I told Kareem that I wanted a divorce; I would never submit to the humiliation of his taking another wife. Kareem replied that divorce would be out of the question unless I chose to give up my children for his second wife to raise. He would never allow them to leave his home.

In a flash, I saw my life before me. Kareem, far removed from the dignity and decency of a civilized man, assuming one wife after another. Most men and women sense the limits they can bear; philosophically, I did not have the disposition to abide such debauchery.

Kareem could mouth any deception he chose; but I understood the implications of his taking a second wife. The desire for children was not his real reason. The issue was primitive. We had been wed for eight years; sexual licence was his aim. Obviously, my husband was weary of eating the same dish and sought a new exotic fare for his palate.

To think that Kareem thought me mindless enough to accept his well-thought-out explanation further enraged me. Yes, I would accept what God placed before me, but this dispensation did not extend to my earthly husband. I told Kareem to remove himself from my presence; I would, on this day, refrain from murder.

For the first time, I felt keenly the first emotions of dislike towards my husband. His façade was wisdom and kindness; his very bowels were cunning and selfishness. I had lain beside him eight years; yet he suddenly seemed like a stranger I did not know at all. I asked him to leave my sight. I was disgusted to discover that he was merely a shell of a man with little to commend him after all.

I watched him as he walked away, head low, shoulders slumped. How was it possible to love him less than an hour before? Yet the flow of my love had slowed. I had held the character of Kareem high, regarding him in great favour over other men of our society. Yet, sadly, at the core of his being, he was as all the rest.

Yes, we had lived through a year of difficulties. Yes, marriage proves restrictive and irritating. We had enjoyed seven years of immense pleasures and suffered through only one year of trouble and evolution. For that, thoughts of fresh joys, a new uncomplicated woman perhaps, crept into my partner's dreams.

Worst of all, he was a man who could black-mail the one who had borne his children. Without shame, he had dangled the sinister possibility of his second wife determining the happiness of my precious children. That should connect me with the reality of my male-dominated world.

As a plan began to grow in my mind, I thought of my husband with pity. His memory had dimmed of the fiery one he had wed. Kareem would find it difficult to outwit me in the possession of my children.

Chapter Nineteen

Escape

Unlike most saudi husbands, Kareem kept his family's passports and papers within easy reach of his wife. Already I was a master at duplicating his signature. His personal seal was kept on top of his desk in his home study.

By the time I had gathered my thoughts and returned to the house, Kareem was no longer in evidence. So he was a coward, too. I knew with certainty that he would stay at his father's palace for a night or two.

A sudden thought of Noorah came to mind. I seethed with anger as I imagined my mother-in-law's pleasure at my predicament. More than likely, she had already selected the second wife for her eldest son. Until that moment I had not considered who the new wife would be; perhaps she was a youthful royal cousin, for we royals tend to wed royalty.

I calmly packed a travelling-case and emptied our hidden safe of hundreds of thousands of dollars. Like most of the royals, Kareem had plans for the possibility of revolutionary fervour, which springs to life unexpectedly in lands ruled by monarchies. We had talked of his plan to buy our lives should the populous weak ever overthrow the strong. I uttered a murderous prayer for our Shiite minority in the Eastern Province to overthrow our Sunni leaders; a vision of Kareem's head skewered on a post brought a smile to my grim countenance.

After packing my wealth of jewels in a small travel bag, I prepared my travel papers with utmost ease. Finally I was ready.

I could not trust any of my sisters, for they might be tempted to divulge my plan to their husbands. And men stick together; Kareem would be notified immediately.

I called for my most trusted maid, for I suspected she would be the first questioned by Kareem, and told her I was going to Jeddah for a few days and please to advise my husband of my plans, should he enquire.

I telephoned my favourite of the family's pilots and advised him that we would be flying to Jeddah within the hour; he was to meet me at the airport. I called the servants in Jeddah and informed them that I would be visiting a friend in the city; perhaps I would come by the villa for a visit. Should Kareem call and request to speak to me, they should tell him that I was at the home of a friend and would call him back at my first opportunity.

My deceitful actions were an attempt to keep Kareem from my true travel plans as long as possible.

As I was driven to the airport, I looked in wonder at the mass of Thursday-evening traffic in Riyadh.

Our city was filled with foreign workers, for we Saudis could not bring ourselves to work at menial jobs. One day the underprivileged would weary of our ill-treatment; our carcasses would make food for the packs of wild dogs that roamed our cities.

When the American pilot saw the black shadow that was me walking in his direction, he grinned and waved. He had taken me on many journeys, and was a warm reminder of the open and friendly pilots who had flown my mother and me to Sara's side so many years before. The memory caused my heart to flutter and to ache for the healing embrace of my mother.

When I boarded the plane, I told the pilot that our plans had changed; one of the children had become ill in Dubai, and I had just received a telephone call from Kareem advising me that I should go to our child instead of to Jeddah. He, Kareem, would follow tomorrow if it was a real emergency.

I lied with the greatest of ease when I told the pilot that we, of course, imagined that our youngest was simply homesick and that my presence would soothe her feelings. I laughed when I said that they had been away for three weeks, much too long for the little one.

Without questioning me further, the pilot changed his flight plans. He had flown for our family for many years and knew us as a happy couple. He had no reason to doubt my orders.

Once we arrived in Dubai, I told the pilot to stay at his usual hotel, the Dubai Sheraton. I would call him tomorrow or the day after to advise him of my plans. I told him he should consider himself off duty, for Kareem had said he would not need him or the plane for several days. We owned three Lear jets; one was always on standby for Kareem's use.

The children were ecstatic at the unexpected sight of their mother. The headmaster of the British summer camp shook his head in sympathy when I reported that their grandmother was gravely ill. I would be taking the children, that very night, back with me to Riyadh. He hurried off to his office to locate their passports.

When I shook the man's hand in farewell, I mentioned that I could not locate the servants who had accompanied the children to Dubai. They had not answered the telephone in their room; I imagined they were eating their dinner. Would he call them in the morning and tell them I would have the pilot, Joel, waiting for them at the Dubai Sheraton? They should go immediately and present the pilot with this note. With that, I handed the headmaster an envelope addressed to the American pilot.

In the note I apologized for using him in such a deceptive manner; I added a postscript to Kareem describing how I had duped the pilot. I knew Kareem would have a flash of anger at the pilot, but it would pass when he considered the circumstances. The pilot, Joel, was a favourite of Kareem's. He was sure not to lose his job.

The children and I climbed into the waiting limousine, which sped to the airport; a direct flight to London was departing within the hour. I would use whatever lie I could muster to obtain four seats on the plane.

As it turned out, I did not have to damage my soul with God further. The flight was almost empty; most people were returning to the Gulf at the end of the hot summer, not departing. The children were sleepy and asked few questions; I told them they would be surprised at the end of the journey.

As the children slept, I nervously turned the pages of a magazine. Nothing on the pages penetrated my thoughts; I was considering my next move with great care. The remainder of my life would depend upon the events of the next few weeks. Slowly, the feeling overcame me that someone with a purpose was staring directly at me. Had my flight from Kareem already been discovered?

I looked across the aisle. An Arab woman of thirty or so years of age was staring hard at me. She cradled a sleeping three- or four-year-old girl in her arms. I was relieved to see that my mental intruder was a woman, and a mother, for Saudi men would never have such a one in their employ. Her piercing glower was a puzzle, so I stood, threaded my way around the serving-cart and sat in the empty seat beside her. I asked her what her trouble was. Had I offended her in some manner?

Her granite face came to life, and she practically spat her words at me: 'I was at the airport when you arrived; you and your brood.' She glanced with contempt at my children. 'You practically ran over me and my child as you checked in at the ticket counter!' She looked with black malice into my eyes when she emphasized my nationality in her next insulting sentence: 'You Saudis think you can buy the world!'

My warped day had sapped my strength; I surprised myself even more than I surprised the woman when I burst into tears. Through my sobs, I patted her shoulder and told her I was sorry. I had a great tragedy in my life and catching this flight was of utmost importance. With tears streaming down my face, I returned to my seat.

The woman was of a sympathetic nature, for she was unable to remain far from my side after my show of emotion. She carefully placed her daughter in the seat and knelt in the aisle beside me.

My body stiffened, and I turned away, but she manoeuvred her face close to mine and said: 'Please, I apologize. I, too, have had a great tragedy. If I tell you what happened to my daughter in your country, more than likely at the hands of some of your countrymen, you will understand my great bitterness.'

Having absorbed more horror than most people endure in a lifetime, I felt no desire to carry yet another image of injustice in my mind. Unable to trust my voice, I mouthed the words 'I am sorry'. She seemed to understand that I was on the verge of hysterics so she left my side.

But the woman was unwilling to let the dreadful happening go unheard, and before the flight had ended I knew the cause of her despair. Upon hearing her story, my bitterness further hardened towards the degenerate patriarchal society that endangers all females, even children, who dare to tread on the soil of Saudi Arabia, regardless of their nationality.

Widad, the woman, was from Lebanon. Because of the persistence of the heartbreaking civil war of that once-beautiful little country, Saudi Arabia and the Gulf States were overflowing with Lebanese in search of jobs. Widad's husband was one of the fortunate who had been employed as an executive in one of the many booming businesses in Riyadh. After a favourable beginning, he had felt secure enough to bring his wife and young daughter to live in the desert capital.

Widad had been content with her life in Riyadh. The war in Lebanon had taken away any desire to return to the endless shelling and mindless deaths of the innocent. She happily settled herself in a land far different from the one she had known. A spacious villa was rented, furniture was purchased, lives were reassembled. Widad had been most impressed with the lack of crime in our country. With severe punishments meted out to those guilty, few criminals ply their trade in Saudi Arabia, for a convicted thief will lose his hand, and a murderer or rapist his head. With a mind at peace, she had failed to caution her young daughter of the danger of strangers.

Two months before, Widad had given a small women's party for a group of friends. As with Saudi women, there is little for foreign women to occupy themselves in my land. Widad served light refreshments, and her guests played cards. Two of the women had brought children, so Widad's daughter was fully entertained in the garden.

After the last guest had departed, Widad helped her two Indian servants to clear the house for her husband's return in the evening. The phone rang, and Widad chatted much longer than she had realized. When she glanced through the window, she could see only darkness. She called out for one of the servants to go and bring in her child.

Widad's daughter was not to be found. After a frantic investigation, the last guest remembered that the child had been sitting on the kerb holding her doll. Widad's husband returned, and a search of the neighbourhood was begun. No-one had seen the child.

After weeks of searching, Widad and her husband could only surmise that their sole child had been abducted and more than likely murdered. When all hope for her precious daughter was gone, Widad found she could no longer reside in her villa in Riyadh. She returned to her family in war-torn Lebanon. To earn a living for them, her husband remained in his job, in the same villa.

Ten days after Widad arrived in Beirut, she heard a loud pounding on her apartment door. Frightened by the recent militia battles in her neighbourhood, she pretended that no-one was at home until she heard the voice of her neighbour screaming news from her husband in Riyadh.

The neighbour had just received a telephone call from Widad's husband. The line had been disconnected, but not before he had taken down an unbelievable message for Widad. She was to take the boat to Cyprus and go immediately to the Saudi embassy in that country. Her visa for re-entry to Saudi Arabia was waiting. She should return as quickly as possible to Riyadh. Their daughter was alive! She had come home.

Three long days were needed for the boat trip from Jounieh in Lebanon to Larnaca in Cyprus, so that her visa could be stamped, and then the plane trip to Riyadh. By the time Widad arrived in Riyadh, the startling truth of their child's whereabouts was revealed.

Once Widad's husband had recovered from the shock of driving up to his villa to find his long-lost daughter standing by the gate, he had taken the child to a clinic to ascertain if she had been raped, for that was his biggest fear. After a thorough examination, the discovery was chilling. The physician told the astonished father that his child had not suffered from sexual assault. However, she had recently undergone major surgery. Widad's daughter had been used as a kidney donor, the doctor told him. The child's scars were ragged, and infection had set in from filth.

Speculations were wild among the medical staff that examined the child, for many questions arose as to donor-typing and surgical procedures. It was unlikely that the child had undergone surgery in Saudi Arabia; at that time such an operation was not common in the kingdom.

When the police investigated, they suggested that the child had been taken to India by a rich

Saudi who had a child in need of a kidney transplant. Perhaps this person had abducted more than one child and had selected the one most suitable. No-one could determine the events that led to the surgery, for the child could only recall a long black car and a bad-smelling handkerchief held by a big man. She had awakened to severe pain. Isolated in a room with a nurse who could not speak English, she saw no other persons. The day of her release, she was blindfolded, driven for a long time and unexpectedly dropped at her door.

Without a doubt, whoever had abducted the child was wealthy, for when her father had jumped from the car and seized his daughter in his arms she was clutching a small bag filled with more than twenty thousand dollars in cash, along with many pieces of expensive jewellery.

Understandably, Widad despised my land and the oil riches that had shaped a people who considered their wealth the conqueror of all of life's obstacles. Sacred body parts were taken from innocent children and cash left to neutralize the anger of those injured! When Widad saw my look of utter disbelief at her story, she rushed to bring me her sleeping child and exposed the long red scar that showed clearly the moral depths to which some men will stoop.

I could only shake my head in horror.

Widad gazed at her sleeping daughter with rapt love; her return was nothing short of a miracle. Widad's parting words erased the fragile pride I still had left in my nationality: 'You, as a Saudi woman, have my sympathy. In my short time in your country, I saw the manner of your lives. For sure, money may smooth your paths, but such a people as the Saudis will not endure.' She paused for a moment of reflection before continuing: 'While it is true that financial desperation leads foreigners to Saudi Arabia, you are still hated by all that have known you.'

I last saw Widad at Heathrow, clinging fiercely to her precious child. After scheduled medical appointments for her daughter in London, Widad was willing to risk the bombs of Lebanese enemies over the hypocrisy and inconceivable evil of those of my land, the Saudis.

The children and I stayed overnight in London. We crossed the Channel by ferry and arrived in France the following day. From there we went by train to Zurich. I left the children in a hotel for a few hours while I emptied my son's Swiss bank account. With a draft for more than six million dollars in hand, I felt secure.

I hired a chauffeur-driven car to take us to Geneva; from there we flew back to London and then on to the Channel Islands. There, I deposited the money in an account in my name and kept the cash from the safe in Riyadh for our expenses. We then flew to Rome, where I hired another driver to take us back to Paris.

In Paris, I hired a full-time housekeeper, a driver and a bodyguard. Then, under an assumed name, I rented a villa on the outskirts of Paris. After such a confusing trail, I felt secure that Kareem would never find us.

A month later, I left the children in the care of the housekeeper while I flew to Frankfurt. There, I entered a bank and said that I was from Dubai and wanted to make a large deposit. Escorted into the bank manager's office and given preferential treatment, I removed large sums of money from my bag and laid the cash upon the manager's desk.

While he stared in shock at the money, I said that I needed to make a telephone call to my husband, who was away on business in Saudi Arabia. I was, of course, more than willing to pay for the call and laid five hundred dollars in his hand. The manager quickly got to his feet and practically clicked his heels together as he told me to take as much time as I needed. He closed the door and said he would be three offices down the hallway if I needed him.

I telephoned Sara. I knew her baby had been born by now, and she would more than likely be at home. I breathed a sigh of relief when one of the servants answered and said yes, the mistress was at home.

Sara screamed in relief when she heard my voice. I quickly asked her if her telephone lines were tapped, and she said she was not certain. In a rush of words she added that Kareem was out of his mind with worry. He had traced me from Dubai to London, but had lost all evidence of us from that point. He told the family what had happened and was truly filled with deep regret. He wanted nothing more than for me and the children to come home. Kareem had said we must talk.

I asked Sara to give my husband a brief message. I wanted him to know that I found him despicable; he would never see us again. Furthermore, I had made arrangements for citizenship for the children and me in another country. Once I was fully protected in a new land, I would advise my sisters of my new life, but Kareem must never know where I was. And, as an added worry for Kareem, I told Sara to let him know that Abdullah, his son, no longer wanted contact with his father.

With that, I left the subject of Kareem behind. With delight, I learned that Sara had a new baby son and that the rest of my family was in good health. She said Father and Ali were furious and insisted I return to Riyadh and adhere to Kareem's every wish, as was my duty. I had expected nothing more from those two of my very blood.

Sara tried to soothe me and asked if it would not be better to accept a new wife rather than to live my life as a refugee. I asked her if she would consider such an arrangement with Asad. Her silence was my answer.

After the call was made, I shoved my money back into my bag and slipped out of the bank without further notice from the eager manager. I felt a twinge of regret for my trickery, yet I knew I could not risk a call from a payphone, for an operator might well announce the country calling to hidden tape machines linked to Kareem.

In deep contemplation of Sara's words, I felt a smile spread across my face. My plan was working.

But I thought it best to let Kareem suffer additional agony. He would need some time to recognize that I would never accept the multiple-wife existence, no matter the ultimate price.

Actually, the children knew nothing of the drama in our lives. I had told them a convincing tale of their father's business taking him to the Orient for many months. Instead of remaining in Riyadh to suffer boredom, he had thought we would enjoy a pleasant time in the French countryside. Abdullah was curious as to why he received no calls from his father, but I kept him occupied with his lessons and numerous social activities; young minds adapt more easily than we could ever imagine. Our two daughters were still babies unable to consider dire circumstances. They had spent their lives travelling; the missing link was the absence of their father. I did my best to compensate.

I consoled myself by considering the alternatives. Life for my children in Riyadh with their parents in constant turmoil was unacceptable in my mind. Life without their mother would be unnatural. For if Kareem brought another woman into our lives the murder of my husband was a real possibility. What good would I be to the children without my head, for it would surely be parted from my body after I took the life of their father! For a moment I considered the sharp blade of the executioner's sword and shuddered at the thought that I might one day feel that coldness. I knew I was fortunate to be a royal, for I, like Ali so many years ago, could ease through difficult legal and ethical situations without the interference of the men of religion. Were I not of royal blood, the pounding of stones would end my life for such actions. But we royals keep our scandals inside our walls; no-one outside the family would know of my defection. Only Kareem could call for my death; and, no matter what my actions, I knew with certainty that my husband did not have the stomach to call for my blood.

I called Sara once a month. During this lengthy absence from my family and country, my days and nights were restless. But I knew there was gain to be had; my determination and patience would alter Kareem's plans of cluttering our lives with other wives.

Five months after my departure I agreed to speak with Kareem over the telephone. I flew to London to place the call. Our conversation convinced me that Kareem was desperate with desire to see me and the children. He would now enter the second stage of my carefully laid trap.

We made plans to meet in Venice the following weekend. My husband was stunned to see me accompanied by four hefty German bodyguards. I told Kareem I no longer trusted his word; he might have hired thugs to kidnap me and bundle me off to Riyadh to face the unjust way our legal system dealt with disobedient wives! His face began to redden. He swore he blushed with shame; I thought perhaps he was angered by his inability to control his wife.

Our impasse ended with a compromise. I would return to Riyadh only if Kareem signed a legal document stating that so long as he and I were wed he would not take another wife. If he were to break his word, I was to be given a divorce, custody of our children, and half of his fortune. In addition, I was to retain, under my control, the money I had taken out of our son's account in Switzerland. Kareem would replace Abdullah's funds. In addition, he would deposit a million dollars in each of our daughters' names in a Swiss bank account. I would keep in my possession our passports with updated papers stating we could travel without restrictions.

I told Kareem that after he signed the necessary papers I would remain in Europe with the children for an additional month. He had been warned of my determination; perhaps his desire for me would fade after consideration. I was not interested in replaying the same song twice. Kareem winced at my words, delivered with a hardness he had seldom heard.

I accompanied Kareem to the airport. My husband was not a happy man. I walked away less content than I had anticipated after the biggest gamble of my life had produced such a stunning victory. I had found that there is little joy derived from forcing a man to do what is right.

One month later I called Kareem to hear his decision. He confessed that I was his strength, his life. He wanted his family back, with everything as it was before. I bluntly told him that surely he could not expect to sever our love with the cold knife of indifference and then expect that a seamless union would remain in our grasp. We had been among the most fortunate of couples with love, family and unlimited wealth. He was the destroyer of all that, not I.

I returned to Riyadh. My husband was waiting, with trembling lips and a hesitant smile. Abdullah and my daughters went wild with joy at seeing their father. My pleasure slowly grew from the happiness of my children.

I found I was a stranger in my home, listless and unhappy. Too much had happened for me to go back to the Sultana of a year ago. I needed a real purpose, a challenge. I decided I would return to school; there were now colleges for women in my country. I would discover normal life and leave behind the mindless routines of a royal princess.

As far as Kareem was concerned, I could only wait for time to erase the bad memories of his behaviour. I had undergone a transition in the fight to save my marriage from the alien presence of another woman. Kareem had been the supreme figure in my life until he weakened our union with talk of wedding another. A substantial part of our love was destroyed. Now he was simply the father of my children and little more.

Kareem and I set about rebuilding our nest and providing our children with the tranquillity we so valued for our young. He said he keenly felt the loss to our love. He valiantly tried to redeem himself in my eyes. He said that if I continued to sit in judgement of his past behaviour we and the children might well lose the enjoyment of our future. I said little but knew it was true.

The trauma of our personal war was past, but the taste of peace was far from sweet. I reflected often on the emotional scars I had acquired in such a short lifetime; sadly, all my wounds had been inflicted by men. As a result, I could hold not even one member of the opposite sex in high esteem.

Chapter Twenty

The Great White Hope

Suddenly it was August 1990.

A glittering dinner-party was in progress at our villa in Jeddah when we heard the horrifying news that two of our neighbours were locked in a deadly struggle across the border in the tiny country of Kuwait. Kareem and I were entertaining twenty guests from our exclusive circle when the news was shouted out from the top of the stairwell by our son, Abdullah, who had been listening to the BBC on his shortwave radio. After a long dry silence, a disbelieving roar rose throughout the room.

Few Saudis, even those royals involved in the negotiations between Kuwait and Iraq, had really believed that Saddam Hussein would invade Kuwait. Kareem had been present at the conference that ended in a stalemate on that very day, 1 August 1990, in Jeddah. The crown prince of Kuwait, Sheikh Saud Al Abdullah Al Salem Al Sabah, had just returned to Kuwait with the hope that war could be averted.

When our son cried out that Iraqi troops were advancing on Kuwait City, the seriousness of the attack was evident. I wondered if the huge family of Al Sabah would escape with their lives. As a mother, my thoughts were with the innocent children.

I watched Kareem's face across the crowded room. Underneath his calm façade, he was furious. The Iraqis had gone against their word; as a result, the leaders of our government had played a role in minimizing the danger. His brown eyes had a glow that caused a shiver to run down my spine. I knew that he, along with other Al Sa'uds present, would soon leave for a hastily called family conference.

I had heard Kareem speak often of the barbarity of the Baath regime in Iraq. He had said many times that the Iraqis were by nature aggressive and prone to violence in their private lives. He thought that might explain their national acquiescence in a brutal police state.

I myself knew little of the true politics of the area, for Saudi news is heavily censored and our men reveal little of their political activities to their wives. But Kareem's opinion was justified by a story I had heard from an Iraqi. Several years ago, while dining out in London, Kareem, Asad, Sara and I had listened in complete fascination as a casual Iraqi acquaintance bragged of killing his father over a misunderstanding over money.

The son had sent the father his earnings from an investment in Paris. The widowed father had become enamoured with a village woman and had spent the son's earnings on the purchase of expensive gifts for his mistress. When the son returned to Iraq on a visit, he discovered that his money had been squandered. He knew what he had to do, which was to shoot his father dead.

With a loud shout, Kareem had protested at the unbelievable act. The Iraqi was surprised at my husband's bewilderment and disbelief, and responded: 'But he had spent my money! It was mine!' As far as the man was concerned, he had had a reasonable cause to take the life of his father.

His act was so unthinkable and repulsive to Kareem that, departing from his usual mild manner, he jumped towards the man and told him to leave our table. The Iraqi left in a rush. Kareem muttered that such attitudes were not uncommon in Iraq, but social acceptance of murdering one's father found great doubt in his mind.

Kareem, like all Saudi men, revered his father and showed him much respect. He would not think of raising his voice or even presenting his back to his father. I had seen Kareem leave a room backwards on numerous occasions.

Like most Arabs, I am sorry to acknowledge, I am a heavy smoker, yet I was never allowed to smoke in front of Kareem's father.

Kareem, as a member of an outdated monarchy, was acutely interested in the movements of the Middle East that had ousted royals from their throne. As Arab history unfolded, kings were unceremoniously dumped, and quite a number had ended with their bodies riddled with bullet holes. As a royal, Kareem felt fear at the possibility of unrest visiting our land.

In addition, like most Arabs, Kareem felt great shame at the never-ending spectacle of Muslim fighting Muslim. For the most part, we Saudis laid down our arms when our country was bonded from the land of tribes to a kingdom united. Bloodletting is not the manner our men choose to fight our enemies; purchasing power is considered the civilized method of victory.

But, for now, our lives were erupting with the insanity of the drama of real war. While our men rushed to intrude on the momentous decisions of diplomacy, we women called for Abdullah to bring his radio to the sitting-room. The news was sparse, but appeared to be going from bad to worse for the unfortunate Kuwaitis. Before we retired, we learned that Kuwait was occupied; our country was being invaded by thousands of refugees. We Saudis felt ourselves out of harm's way and gave no thought to our personal safety or to danger for our country.

The following week would shake our confidence in our observations. As Saddam's soldiers drew near to our borders, rumours filled our country that he had in mind to swallow two neighbours in one meal!

Streams of Saudis joined the Kuwaitis in the exodus from the eastern area of our country. We received frantic telephone calls from nervous family members with the news that Riyadh was crowded with thousands of panicked people. Soon, many Saudis felt Riyadh to be unsafe; the planes and roads to Jeddah were jammed. Madness had erupted in our quiet kingdom.

Sara and I were thrilled to hear that Kuwaiti

women, who are allowed to drive and go unveiled, were even driving down our roads and into the streets of our capital. No Western women could ever imagine our mixed emotions. We were crashing into a storm and, while our glee was mixed with wonder, at the same moment we were frothing with jealousy that our Arab sisters were driving cars and exposing their naked faces in our land! Were our essentials of life, the veil and Saudi customs, now considered nothing more than clutter so easily dismissed in the heat of hostility? Life had been easy for these Kuwaiti women, in stark contrast with our heavy endurance of male mastery. The sting of envy bubbled through our veins. While sympathetic to these women who had lost their country, their homes and loved ones, we were undeniably swollen with resentment at the ones who had exposed the ridiculousness of our puritanical situation. How we hungered for the rights they had assumed with such ease!

There was a rumour a minute in those dark days of August. When Kareem told me that the latest rumour was true, that our king had agreed for foreign troops to travel to our land, I knew our lives would never again be the same.

With the arrival of the American troops, Saudi feminists' most ambitious dreams felt the spark of life. No Saudi had ever imagined seeing women in military uniforms, guarding that ultimate bastion of male dominance that is Saudi Arabia. It was unthinkable! Our men of religion were aghast and spoke with heavy tidings of the coming harm to our land.

The disruption to our lives can never be measured. No earthquake could have shaken us more.

While I was happy at the turn of events, and felt the change would be beneficial, many Saudi women raged with contempt. There were those I deemed silly who fretted with the possibility of these foreign women stealing their husbands! I suppose such a worry was real, for most Saudi women endure their husbands' trips abroad with trepidation, few believing their spouses would remain faithful in the midst of Western blonde temptations. Many of my friends reassured themselves with the thought that only a prostitute or a woman with little else to promote herself would consider such degradation as shared living-quarters with strange men. Saudi women whispered that they had read that these American women were allowed in the armies solely to service the men and keep them from sexual deprivation.

Our emotions were in conflict over these super-women who came and went at will in a country not their own. We had known little of American female soldiers, for our country censors all news of women who control their destiny from the citizens of Saudi Arabia. And during our infrequent travels abroad our paths led us to shopping districts, not military bases. When Asad brought Sara uncensored copies of American and European magazines and newspapers, we were astonished to see that the women soldiers were quite attractive. Many were mothers.

Our understanding could not let us imagine such freedom. Our modest goals involved only the acts of uncovering our faces, driving and working. Our land now harboured those of our sex perfectly prepared to meet men in battle.

We women of Arabia were on an emotional roller-coaster. One moment we hated all the foreign women, both Kuwaiti and American, in our land. At the same moment, the Kuwaiti women warmed our hearts with their show of defiance of our centuries-old tradition of male supremacy. While conservative, they had not completely succumbed to the insane social custom of male dominance. Yet moments of jealousy came and went as we realized that they had somehow lifted the status of all Muslim women by their very attitude, while we Saudi women had done little to elevate our lives other than to complain. Where had we gone wrong? How had they managed to discard the veil – and obtain freedom to drive at the same time?

We felt the agony of envy, yet we were ecstatic, too. Confused at the happenings around us, we women met daily to dissect the shift of attitudes and the sudden universal awakenings to the plight of Saudi women. In the past, few women dared express their desire for reform in Islamic Saudi Arabia, for the hope of success was so dim and the penalties too severe for challenging the status quo. After all, our country is the home of Islam; we Saudis are the 'keepers of the faith'. To cover our shame at our forced repressions, we spoke proudly to our Kuwaiti sisters of our unique heritage: we Saudi women hold high the symbols of Muslim belief the world over. Then, suddenly, middle-class Saudi women threw down their shackles. They faced the fundamentalists head-on and called out for the world to free them in the same instant they freed the besieged Kuwaitis!

Sara caused me to tremble when she rushed into the palace screaming. My only thought was that of chemicals invading the air my children were breathing! Had an enemy plane filled with chemical bombs escaped the detection of the forces guarding our land? I stood still, holding my breath, undecided as to where to go or what to do. Any moment I would more than likely be writhing on the floor, thinking my last thoughts. I cursed myself! I should have followed Kareem's wishes and taken our young ones to London, far from the possibility of a painful slow death for those I had carried in my womb.

Sara's words finally penetrated my fear, and the news she told rung as a celebration in my ears. Asad had just called her; Saudi, yes *Saudi*, women were actually driving cars up and down the streets of Riyadh!

I cried out with joy; Sara and I hugged and danced. My youngest daughter began to sob in fear when she came into the room and saw her mother and aunty rolling and screaming on the floor. I soothed her fears when I grabbed her in my arms and assured her our silly nonsense was a result of great happiness; my prayers had been answered.

The American presence was going to alter our lives in a wonderful, wonderful way!

Kareem burst through the door with a dark look in his eyes. He wanted to know what the trouble was; he could hear our cries in the garden.

Did he not know? Women had broken the first of the unyielding barriers – they were claiming their right to drive! Kareem's response sobered our reaction. I knew his opinion on the matter; there is no mention of such in our religion, he would say. He, like many other Saudi men, had always thought it absurd that Saudi women were not allowed to drive.

With a weary tone, my husband now voiced the unthinkable. 'This is exactly the type of action that we did not want you women to take! We have been battling the fanaticals for every concession! Their biggest fear is that our decisions will result in women moving towards more privileges. What is more important to you, Sultana,' he cried out, 'to have soldiers to protect our lives from the Iraqi menace, or to choose this time to drive?'

I was furious with Kareem. Many times he had protested against the silly custom that chains Saudi women to their homes. And now his fear of the men of religion brought his cowardly soul to the surface. How I yearned to be wed to a warrior, a man with the hot flame of righteousness to guide his life.

In a temper, I hotly replied that we women could not be 'beggars with conditions'. What luxury to be able to pick our time and place! We had to take what small opportunities were presented. Now was our time, too, and Kareem should stand by our side. Surely, the throne would not be toppled over the mere fact that women drove in our streets!

My husband was angry at all women at that moment and told me in a hard voice that this incident would delay women's causes for decades. He told us our joy would turn to sorrow when we witnessed the punishment meted out to those so foolish. The proper time will come for women to drive, he warned, but this was not the moment for such drama. His words hung in the air as he made his retreat. A man had spoken!

Kareem had stolen our small moment of pleasure. I hissed like a cat at his back, and Sara's lips trembled as she held back her smile. She dismissed Kareem's words with contempt. She reminded me that the men in our family talked sympathetically about women's rights, but in reality they were little different from the extremists. All men liked a heavy hand on the heads of their women. Otherwise, we would have seen some lifting of our heavy burdens. Our husbands and father were of the royal family that ruled the land; if they could not help us, who could?

'The Americans!' I said with a smile. 'The Americans.'

Kareem's words proved to be true. The forty-seven brave young women who demonstrated against the informal ban on driving became the scapegoats of every grievance the *mutawas* considered. They were women of the middle class, women who were teachers of other women or students – our thinkers and doers. As a result of their bravery, their lives were devastated by their actions: passports taken, jobs lost and families harassed.

While shopping in a local mall, Sara and I overheard young religious students as they aroused Saudi men against these women by saying they were leaders of vice and made their living as prostitutes; they had been denounced in the mosque as such by men who had reason to know! My sister and I lingered at a shop window to hear the young men loudly proclaim that the temptations transported from the West would cause the honour of all Saudis to disintegrate!

I wanted to meet the women, to share in their glory. When I proposed my idea to Kareem, his reaction violently closed the possibility. He threatened to have me shut in the house should I attempt such an outrage. At that moment I hated my husband, for I knew he was capable of fulfilling his threat; he was suddenly wild with fear for our country as well as of the havoc we women could bring to the royal family.

Within a few days I built up my courage and tried to locate those brave women. I returned to the mall. When I saw throngs of men in a circle, I told my Filipino driver to go to them and say he was a Muslim (there are a number of Muslim Filipinos in Saudi Arabia) and request the paper with the telephone numbers of the 'fallen women'. He was to say that he wanted to call their fathers or their husbands to protest at the behaviour of their daughters or wives.

He returned with the paper; I warned him against telling Kareem. Fortunately, unlike Arab servants, the Filipinos tend to avoid our family conflicts and make no mention of our small freedoms to our husbands.

The paper listed thirty names and telephone numbers. My hand shook as I dialled the first number. Only three calls were answered in weeks of constant dialling. No matter what I said, I was told that I must have the wrong number. The harassment had been so insistent that the families chose either denial or not to answer their phones.

On his way out of the country, Ali came by to visit. He and his family of four wives and nine children were travelling to Paris for a few weeks. My brother claimed he wanted to fight the Iraqis, but his plate was filled with business responsibilities that were indeed more important to our country than another man in uniform. He, Ali, must do his duty and leave Saudi Arabia.

I knew my brother was going to wait out the war in safety. I had no desire on that day to confront his cowardice; I merely smiled and wished him a good trip.

The topic of the women drivers was introduced when Ali hinted slyly that one of the protesters had been put to death by her father for shaming the family. The father had thought that by executing his daughter, the religious fanatics would leave him and the remainder of the family in peace. Ali actually smiled; how I hated this brother of mine. He was well suited to a land that kept women at his feet. He would fight to the end to keep women in a lowly position, for a man such as he would be terrorized by a woman of strength and character.

When I questioned Kareem, he claimed not to know of the incident, but told me to put it out of my mind. This was not our affair. He mentioned that he would not be surprised, since the families of the women had suffered along with the trouble-makers. He smugly said, 'I told you so,' reminding me of his prediction on the day of the protest. I felt that Kareem had tricked me with his past talk of free women; surely he now was little advanced over Ali in his thinking. Was there not one man in my country who desired women's bonds loosened?

The rumour of the death of the young woman held fast in our land, and to this day her fate has not been denied or confirmed; it hangs over us women, a veiled threat of the ultimate sacrifice awaiting those with courage.

The war we so dreaded came and went. Our men fought and died, but I heard from Kareem that many of our soldiers had not fought bravely. In fact the Allies had found it necessary to invent tactics to ensure that we Arabs were not offended when the truth about our warriors was revealed. My husband blushed when he told of Saudis running away from, instead of towards, the enemy. Our only pride in our military was for the prowess of our pilots, who performed with honour.

Asad gave his opinion that we should not feel

shame but relief at this assessment. A strong military would be a risk to our very heads; the throne could not survive a precise military machine. In the Arab world, a capable military overthrows monarchies; for truly people desire a voice in the policies of their land. Our family had seen such happenings and maintained a family-run organization of men unwilling to fight. Certainly, our ruling family is sly and purposely keeps the Saudi soldier slovenly and far from his peak.

In the end, events of the war served to abort our confidence in legendary social change for the women of Saudi Arabia. The fight that brought forth Western eyes from around the world to probe the disorders of our society ended all too quickly. The fading power of our enemy, Saddam, lifted the interest in our plight and transferred the whispered pledges of help to the distressing predicament of the Kurds, who were languishing in the mountain snows.

At the end of the war, our men tended to their prayers with great diligence, for they had been saved from the threat of invading armies – and free women.

Who is to say which threat gave them the most worry?

Epilogue

The haunting sound that lifts the heart of every Muslim with joy filled the air. The faithful were being called to pray. 'God is great, there are no other Gods, but God; and Muhammad was his Prophet. Come to prayer, come to prayer. God is great; there is no God, but God.'

It was dusk; the big yellow circle that was the sun was slowly sinking. For faithful Muslims, the time had come for the fourth prayer of the day.

I stood on the bedroom balcony and watched my husband and son leave our palace grounds and walk, hand in hand, to the mosque. I saw that many men were gathering, greeting each other with the spirit of brotherhood.

The turbulent memories of my childhood came back to me, and I was a young girl again, shut out from the love exclusive to my father and his treasured son, Ali. Nearly thirty years had passed, yet nothing had changed. My life had come full circle.

Father and Ali, Kareem and Abdullah, yesterday, today and tomorrow, immoral practices passed from father to son. Men I loved, men I detested, leaving a legacy of shame in their treatment of women.

My eyes followed the movements of my beloved flesh, my most precious blood; my husband and son entered the mosque hand-in-hand, without me.

I felt quite the loneliest figure ever to have lived.

Afterword

At the end of the Gulf War of 1991, there was a universal desire for peace to come to the turbulent Middle East. Endless proposals from leaders of many nations were presented to those in power in an effort to end the interminable violence in this part of the world.

Along with a desire for peace, many who care about the Middle East and its people yearned for change in ancient traditions that have no religious basis yet serve to bind the women of the Middle East to the whims of the men who sired or wed them. While the reality of lasting peace gains momentum in the diplomatic moves of President George Bush, the elusive dream of freedom for women in Arabia languishes. Western men in power have little interest in holding high the banner of justice for ones without political prestige; that is, women.

The Gulf War to free Kuwait also turned out to be a war of sharply growing conflict between the men and women of Arabia. Where women saw hope for social change, men felt the danger of any change in a society that differed little from what it was two centuries ago. Husbands, fathers and sons were unwilling to challenge radical religious forces for women's rights. The cause of freedom for women in Arabia withered in a backlash from religious extremists, for the arrival of foreign troops had unleashed their power. The promise of bitter strife from the men of religion spread fear throughout the land. Sadly, in 1992, Sultana, along with other Saudi women, has been forced to retreat to the trenches of yesterday.

Surprisingly, the rich and powerful, for the first time, are now targeted by the religious police and are suffering raids and arrests like other Saudis. Ordinary citizens, instead of being concerned over the loss of freedom for all citizens, laugh with abandon at the thought of the royals and rich citizens enduring the same fierce scrutiny from the *mutawas* that they themselves have always known. Freedom to drive, to toss aside the veil, to travel without permission are lost dreams among more life-threatening concerns such as the growing menace of regional religious extremists. Who knows when another opportunity with such potential for social change as a war will come for the women of Arabia?

As modern societies strive to improve the living conditions of all peoples, women throughout the world still face the authentic threat of torture or death under the primitive control of the male sex. The seams of the cloak of female slavery are sewn with the strong thread of male resolve to cling to their historic power over women.

In the spring of 1983 I met a Saudi woman

who has changed my life for ever. You know her as Sultana. Our mutual attraction and desire for friendship flourished, for almost instantly we were in harmony. Sultana's passion for life and her amazing mental capacity altered my Westerner's incorrect perceptions of the 'women in black', whom at that time I viewed as an incomprehensible species of the human race.

As an American who had lived among the Saudis since 1978, I had met and socialized with many Saudi women. But, to my foreign eyes, all presented the same tainted mask of defeat. Life for the rich merchant class, or the royal family of the cities to which they belonged, was too comfortable to shift the delicate balance of their lives. The bedouin women of the villages bore their intolerable life with surprising dignity. Indeed, upon meeting me, they moaned in sympathy for one such as I who was 'forced' to venture out into the cruel world on my own, without the protection or guidance of a man. 'Haram [What a pity],' they would say, while patting my shoulder and expressing their despair for one such as I. Behind the veneer of contentment or sympathy, the truth of their condition was concealed.

Sultana exposed me to the vociferous wrath that borders on despair in the minds of many Saudi women hidden behind the veil. With this new perspective, I became convinced that Saudi women did little to influence Saudi culture; instead Saudi culture had created them.

In the autumn of 1988, Sultana approached me

with the request that I, her friend, write her life-story. Much had transpired in her young life and in the lives of other Saudi women of her acquaintance that deserved redress, she believed. But my common sense prevailed. I expressed my doubt of the ultimate advantage such a risky endeavour would bring for her. Other thoughts of my personal interests came to mind and valid excuses for my pacifism sprang to my lips: I loved the Middle East; my dearest friends were in the area; I knew numerous happy Saudi women.

My doubt and denial had no end, for I had personally wearied of the constant criticism by Western journalists of the land I now called my home. Undeniably, the isolation of the Muslims sprouted from endless negative reports from the world's press. An overabundance of articles and books censorious of the Middle East were already in print; I did not want to join the common pattern of 'Arab-bashing', committed by many who took shelter under the economic umbrella of the oil-rich land.

I told Sultana: 'No, I do not wish to condemn.' My desire was to show the Arabs in the favoured light of understanding, to point out their kindness, hospitality and generosity.

Sultana, the princess feminist, forced my eyes upon the naked truth. While it is true that much good thrives in Saudi Arabia, there could be no celebration of life in this society until its women were free to live without fear. Sultana pointed out the conspicuous: 'Jean, as a woman, your loyalties are misplaced!' Sultana could not face defeat: she continued to expound upon the reality of the corruption of her own sex. She was a better woman than I. She did not flinch from risk of life or limb for the cause she sought.

As is the story of her life, Sultana overcame all obstacles, including my stubborn resistance. After I made the difficult decision to collaborate with her to write her story, I knew in my heart that I could have taken no other course. The Christian West and the Islamic East are knitted together by a bond that can withstand the fear I felt in the conception of this undertaking. This was a book that was meant to be.

Much has been sacrificed by many people in the writing of this book: peace of mind for the safety of Sultana and her family; fear for friends still in Arabia who have no knowledge of the existence of this book; but, most of all, I face the loss of the love, support and companionship of Sultana, the person who has thrilled and inspired me with her fiery spirit. For the sad fact is, the moment this publication becomes common knowledge, our paths can no longer cross. My dearest friend will be locked away from me behind the darkness of silence. This is our loving mutual decision, I should add. To reveal our association would ensure grave punishment for many people; most of all, for Sultana.

At our final meeting, in August 1991, a feeling of perverse futility mired my joy, while I marvelled at Sultana's wave of optimism. She felt joyous hope at the outcome of our endeavour and declared that she would rather perish than live as one conquered. Her words gave me strength for the approaching storm: 'Until these despicable facts are made public, there can be no help; this book is like the first steps of a baby who could never run without that first brave attempt to stand on its own. Jean, you and I will stir the ashes and start a fire. Tell me, how can the world come to our aid if it does not hear our cry? I feel it deep in my soul; this is the beginning of change for our women.'

Many years of my adult life were spent living in the Middle East. For three years, I have been reading and rereading Sultana's notes and diaries. Clandestine meetings have been held with her in many of the major capitals of the world. I have shown her the final manuscript, which she read with great delight – and pain. After Sultana read the final sentence of this book, my friend began to weep. When she composed herself, she said I had perfectly captured her spirit, her life's experiences, as clearly as if I had been by her side, as indeed I had for many years. She then asked that I fill in the blanks of her life not covered in her diaries. Here is what Sultana wants you to know.

Sultana's father still lives. He maintains four wives and four palaces in his six favourite cities throughout the world. He has many young children from his youthful wives. Sadly, his relationship with Sultana has not been tempered by age. He rarely visits any of his daughters, but takes great pride in his sons and grandsons.

Ali has not experienced maturity, and his habits remain much the same as those of a spoiled child. His streaks of cruelty are reserved for his female children, whom he treats as he saw his sisters managed by his father. Today, Ali has four wives and countless mistresses. Recently, he was chastised by the king for excessive corruption, but no action was taken to curb his behaviour.

Sara and Asad have maintained their wedded bliss. As of this date, they are the parents of five lively children. Who knows if Huda's prediction of six will come true? Only Sara, of all Sultana's sisters, knows of the existence of this book.

The remainder of Sultana's sisters and their families are well.

Omar was killed in a car accident on the road to Dammam. His family in Egypt is supported by Sultana's father.

Randa's father purchased a villa in the south of France, where Randa now lives most of the year. She has not remarried after being divorced by Sultana's father. There is a rumour in the family that Randa has a French lover, but there is doubt if this is true.

Sultana never again heard from Wafa; she imagines her in a village surrounded by a large number of children, leading the life so dreaded by educated young women in Saudi Arabia.

Marci returned to the Philippines and realized her life's ambition as Sultana knew she would. She worked as a nurse for a while in Riyadh, but once wrote Sultana a letter outlining her plans to take a

296

job in Kuwait; restrictions in Saudi Arabia were too severe to tolerate, she said. Sultana has not heard from Marci since. She fervently hopes that Marci was not raped or killed during the Iraqi invasion, the fate of many beautiful young women.

Huda died years ago. She was buried in the sands of Arabia, far from her native land of Sudan.

Saddest of all, Sameera remains locked in the woman's room. Tahani heard two years ago that Sameera had gone mad. The servants reported that she had screamed for days on end and finally began to speak in a gibberish that none could understand. They occasionally hear her sobbing, and the food-tray is emptied daily, so she still lives. The family swears that the girl will be released when the old man of the family dies, but he is in fine health even at an old age. In any case, it is thought that freedom will no longer benefit Sameera.

Sultana received her master's degree in philosophy two years ago. She does not work at her profession, but says the knowledge she acquired has given her an inner peace and a feeling of oneness with the world. In her studies, she discovered that many other peoples have survived grave injustices. Human progress is indeed slow, she has found, but brave souls continue to push forward, and she is proud to be one of them.

Kareem and Sultana are settled into a relationship that is bound by custom and the mutual love of their children. She regrets that their love never fully revived after the incident of the second wife.

Six years ago Sultana was stricken with a venereal

disease; after much distress, Kareem admitted that he participated in a weekly adventure of sex with strangers. Several of the high-ranking princes send a weekly plane to Paris to pick up prostitutes for a trip to Saudi Arabia. A madam then selects the most beautiful girls from all around the world who ply their trade in France. Each Tuesday they board a plane to Arabia; the following Monday the weary prostitutes are flown out. Kareem told of special palaces in the major cities of Saudi Arabia that house up to a hundred prostitutes. Most of the high-ranking princes of the royal family are invited to participate and to feel free to select any of the women. For these men, women continue to exist only as objects of pleasure or as a vehicle to provide sons.

After the scare of the disease, Kareem promised he would avoid the weekly tryst, but Sultana says she knows that he is weak in the face of such a feast, and that he continues to indulge himself without shame. Their wonderful love has vanished except in memory; Sultana says she will stand with her husband and continue her struggle for the sake of her daughters.

Sultana says that the saddest aspect of her life continues to be watching the black forms of her two young daughters, now wrapped in the black cloaks and veils that, after all the years of rebellion, still cling to a new generation of young women in Saudi Arabia. As always, primitive customs determine women's roles in Saudi society.

The presence of the American troops during the

Gulf War that gave such hope of freedom for Sultana has only brought the *mutawas* greater strength; they now boast of ruling the king who occupies the throne.

Sultana asked that I tell the reader this. Her defiant spirit still rebels through the pages of this book. But her rebellion must be kept in secret; for, although she has the heart for all of life's trials, she could not face the possibility of losing her precious children. Who knows what punishment might be meted out to the one who speaks out truthfully about the hidden lives of women in the land of the two holiest shrines of Islam?

Sultana's destiny was formed in January 1902 when her grandfather Abdul Aziz fought and regained the lands of Saudi Arabia. A dynasty was born. Princess Sultana Al Sa'ud will remain by the side of her husband, Prince Kareem Al Sa'ud, in the Royal House of Al Sa'ud of the Kingdom of Saudi Arabia.

Appendix A

The Laws of Saudi Arabia

The criminal laws of Saudi Arabia adhere to strict Islamic precepts. The word *Islam* means 'surrender to the will of God'. The most important concept of Islam is the Shari'a, or the 'path', which embraces the total way of life ordained by God. All peoples of the Islamic religion are expected to conduct their lives by the traditional values set by Muhammad, the Prophet of God, who was born in AD 570 and died in AD 632.

It is difficult for most Westerners to understand the complete and total submission of Muslims to the laws of the Koran in every aspect of their daily life. The Koran, along with traditions set by Muhammad, is the law of the land in Saudi Arabia.

While living in Saudi Arabia, I once asked a noted scholar of Islam, who made his living as a lawyer, to describe the application of justice in Saudi Arabia that stems from the teachings of the Prophet. His explanations helped dispel my misunderstandings of Saudi law.

Here is a portion of his written report to me that I thought might appeal to the reader's interest:

(1) There are four main sources of the Shari'a: the Koran, which is compiled from thousands of religious verses revealed by God through his Prophet, Muhammad; the Sunna, which are the traditions the Prophet addressed that are not recorded in the Koran; the Ijma, which are the perceptions of the Ulema, or religious scholars; and the Qiyas, which is a method whereby known jurists agree upon new legal principles.

(2) The king of Saudi Arabia is not exempt from the regulations set forth by the Shari'a.

(3) The court system itself is complicated, but if a judgement is taken to appeal it is reviewed by the court of appeals. This court, usually consisting of three members, increases to five members if the sentence imposes death or mutilation. The king is the final arbitrator who serves as a final court of appeal and as a source of pardon.

(4) Crimes are classified into three divisions: Hudud, Tazir and Qisas. Crimes of Hudud are crimes that are denounced by God; the punishment is made known in the Koran. Crimes of Tazir are given to the appropriate authority to determine punishment. Crimes of Qisas give the victim the right to retaliate.

CRIMES OF HUDUD

Crimes of Hudud include theft, drinking of alcohol, defamation of Islam, fornication and adultery.

Persons found guilty of theft are punished by payment of fines, imprisonment, or amputation of the right hand. (The left hand is amputated if the right has already been amputated.)

Persons found guilty of drinking, selling or buying alcohol, sniffing drugs, taking injections of drugs or stirring drugs into dough are punished by a sentence of eighty lashes.

Persons found guilty of defamation of Islam are sentenced according to the circumstances. The harshness of the sentence varies depending on whether the person is a Muslim or a non-Muslim. Flogging is the general punishment for Muslims.

Persons found guilty of fornication are flogged. Men are flogged while standing and women while sitting. The faces, heads and vital organs of the guilty are protected. The usual number is forty lashes, but this number may vary according to the circumstances.

Adultery is the most serious of crimes. If the guilty party is married, he or she is sentenced to death by stoning, beheading or shooting. Stoning is the usual method of punishment. Proof of this crime must be established by confession or by four witnesses to the act.

CRIMES OF TAZIR

The crimes of Tazir are similar to misdemeanour crimes in America. There is no set punishment, but each person is judged on an individual basis, according to the seriousness of the crime and the sorrow shown by the criminal.

CRIMES OF QISAS

If a person is found guilty of crimes against an individual or his family, the aggrieved family has the right to retaliate. The sentence is decided in private by the family, and the actual punishment is carried out in private.

If murder has been committed, the family has the right to kill the murderer in the same method their loved one was murdered, or in any method they choose.

If a member of the family was accidentally killed (such as in a road accident), the family of the deceased may collect 'blood money'. In the past, camels were used as pay for blood money; today the rate of exchange is in currency. There are set damages according to the various circumstances: the payment can be anywhere from 120,000 to 300,000 Saudi riyals ($45,000–80,000). If a woman is killed, the payment is half that of a man.

If a person cuts off another person's body part, the family or the victim may commit the same act upon the guilty party.

WHO MAY TESTIFY IN CRIMINAL PROCEEDINGS

The witness must be deemed sane, the age of an adult, and a Muslim. Non-Muslims may *not* testify in criminal court. Women may not testify unless it is a personal matter that did not occur in the sight of men. Actually, the testimony of a woman is not regarded as fact but rather as presumption. The court may decide whether the testimony is valid according to the circumstances.

WHY WOMEN ARE FORBIDDEN TO
TESTIFY IN CRIMINAL PROCEEDINGS

There are four reasons given why women's testimony is not valid in a Saudi court.

(1) Women are much more emotional than men and will, as a result of their emotions, distort their testimony.

(2) Women do not participate in public life, so they will not be capable of understanding what they observe.

(3) Women are dominated completely by men, who by the grace of God are deemed superior; therefore, women will give testimony according to what the last man told them.

(4) Women are forgetful, and their testimony cannot be considered reliable.

Appendix B

Glossary

abaaya: a long black cloak worn over the clothing of Saudi Arabian women.

Abu Dhabi: a city located in the United Arab Emirates.

Al Sa'ud: the family that rules the kingdom of Saudi Arabia.

Asir: the traditional name for the south-west region of Saudi Arabia.

Baath: a political movement that began in Syria and spread to Iraq. Arab unity is at the centre of its doctrine.

Bahrain: an island nation that is linked to Saudi Arabia by a causeway.

bedouin: the original Arabs, a nomadic desert people.

Dammam: the city in Saudi Arabia where oil was first struck in 1938.

Dar'iyah: the old city of Riyadh.

Dubai: a city located in the United Arab Emirates.

Empty Quarter: the great desert occupying the south-east corner of Saudi Arabia. Its Arabic name is Rub al Khali.

ghutra: the Arabian headdress worn by men.

Haj: the pilgrimage, one of the five pillars of Islam.

The journey to Makkah is the life's ambition of most Muslims. All Muslims are required to make this journey, if they can afford it.

halawa: the ceremony of removing body hair.

Haram: an expression that means 'pity' or 'sympathy'.

Hijaz: the traditional name for the area of western Arabia. Jeddah, located on the Red Sea, is in the Hijaz area.

houmous: an Arabic dish made of chickpeas, usually scooped up with a piece of pitta bread.

Hudud: crimes of a serious nature which are denounced by God in the Koran.

ibn: means 'son of' (Khalid ibn Faisal, son of Faisal).

igaal: the black cord worn on top of the Arabian headdress.

Ijma: perceptions of the Koran by the religious scholars of Islam.

Jeddah: a beautiful city in Saudi Arabia located on the Red Sea. Jeddah is popular with the expatriate population, who swim and dive in the pristine waters.

Jerusalem: the third-holiest city of Islam, now under the control of the Israelis.

Koran: the holy book of the Islamic faith containing the words of God as they were given to the Prophet Muhammad.

Kurds: a transnational ethnic and linguistic group numbering 18 per cent of Iraq's population. Nationalistic, with the aim of forming their own country, this group of people continues to fight for Kurdish autonomy.

kutab: a common group method of teaching girls in Saudi Arabia prior to the days of education for females.

laban: a refreshing buttermilk-like drink common in the Middle East.

Madinah: the second-holiest city of Islam, called 'the city of the Prophet', and burial-place of Prophet Muhammad.

Makkah: the holiest city of Islam, where God revealed His will to Prophet Muhammad. It is the destination of millions of Muslim pilgrims each year.

Malaz: a residential section of Riyadh popular with wealthy Saudis.

Manama: the capital city of Bahrain, an island nation connected to Saudi Arabia by a causeway.

Mena House: a popular hotel in Cairo frequented by tourists.

Mismaak: the fortress in Riyadh used by the Rasheed clan in the battle of 1902 that returned the Al Sa'uds to power.

mutawa: the morals police of Islam.

Najd: the traditional name for central Arabia. Riyadh is located in this region. The inhabitants are generally known for their conservative behaviour. The Al Sa'ud family are Najdis.

Nasiriyah: a residential section of Riyadh inhabited by members of the royal family and exceptionally wealthy Saudis.

Qisas: a crime committed against a person. The victim or the victim's family can retaliate against the one convicted of such a crime.

Qiyas: the method of agreement of new legal principles in Islam.

Ramadan: the Islamic month of fasting when Muslims worldwide celebrate God's gift of the Koran to man.

Riyadh: the capital of Saudi Arabia.

riyal: the Saudi riyal is the currency of Saudi Arabia.

Shari'a: the law of God for those belonging to the Islamic faith.

Shiite: the branch of Islam that split from the Sunni majority over the issue of the Prophet Muhammad's successor.

souq: the native market-place or bazaar.

Sunna: the traditions of the Islamic faith as addressed by Prophet Muhammad.

Sunni: the majority orthodox branch of Islam. Saudi Arabia is 95 per cent Sunni.

Suras: the chapters of the Koran. There are 114 Suras.

Taif: a mountain-resort village in Saudi Arabia located near Makkah.

Tazir: crimes of misdemeanour under Islamic law.

thobe: a long shirt-like garment worn by Saudi men. Traditionally, the *thobe* is made of white cotton, but during the cool winter months men often wear a *thobe* of a heavier fabric and a darker colour. (As soon as a male child can walk, he is dressed in a tiny *thobe* and head-dress identical to his father's.)

Ulema: Islamic religious scholars who regulate religious life in Saudi Arabia.

Yemen: a country located in the south-west corner of the Arabian peninsula. In the past, Yemenis provided much of Saudi Arabia's manual labour force. When the government of Yemen remained loyal to Saddam Hussein during the Gulf War, most Yemeni labourers were expelled from the kingdom.

Appendix C

Chronology

570   Prophet Muhammad is born in Makkah, Saudi Arabia.

610   Prophet Muhammad sees a vision from God proclaiming him to be the messenger of God. Islam is born.

622   Prophet Muhammad flees an angry mob in Makkah and escapes to Madinah. This flight is forever after known as 'the Hegira', the great crisis of Muhammad's mission on earth. The Muslim calendar begins on that date and is called Hegira in honour of that journey.

632   Prophet Muhammad dies in Madinah.

650   The sayings of Prophet Muhammad are collected and written down. Known as the Koran, this book, which recorded the word of God as told by Muhammad, became the holy book of Muslims.

1446   The first documented Al Sa'ud, ancestor of Sultana, leaves the nomadic life of the desert and settles in Dar'iyah (old Riyadh).

1744   Muhammad Al Sa'ud establishes a

partnership with Muhammad Al Wahhab, a teacher who believes in the strictest interpretation of the Koran. Combined forces of a warrior and a teacher unleash a rigid system of punishment upon the people.

1802–6 Sons of Muhammad Al Sa'ud and Muhammad Al Wahhab, inspired by the teachings of the Koran, attack and capture Makkah and Madinah. They are ruthless, massacring the entire male population of Taif, a settlement above Makkah. With this victory, most of Arabia unites under one authority.

1843–65 The Sa'uds extend authority southwards to Oman.

1876 Sultana's grandfather, Abdul Aziz ibn Sa'ud, founder of the kingdom, is born.

1887 The city of Riyadh is captured by the Rasheeds.

1891 The Al Sa'ud clan flees Riyadh into the Empty Quarter.

1893–4 The Al Sa'ud clan marches across the desert to Kuwait.

1901 *September*. Abdul Aziz, now twenty-five years old, along with his warriors, leaves Kuwait for Riyadh.

1902 *January*. Abdul Aziz and his men capture Riyadh. The new Al Sa'ud dynasty begins.

1915 Abdul Aziz Al Sa'ud enters into an agreement with the British government to receive £5,000 per month to fight the Turks.

1926 Sultana's father is born.

1932 Unification of the dual kingdoms of Hijaz and Najd. Named the Kingdom of Saudi Arabia, it becomes the twelfth-largest country in the world.

1933 Sultana's mother, Fadeela, is born.
May. The United States of America wins concessions (over the British) to search for oil in Saudi Arabia.

1934 Saudi Arabia goes to war against Yemen; peace is established one month later.
15 May. In revenge for the Yemen war, King Abdul Aziz is attacked at the holy mosque in Makkah by three knife-wielding Yemenis. His eldest son, Sa'ud, flings himself in front of his father and is wounded instead.

1938 *20 March*. Oil is discovered in Dammam, Saudi Arabia.

1939 War in Europe halts oil production.

1944 Oil production in the kingdom rises to 8 million barrels a year.

1945 *14 February*. President Roosevelt meets King Abdul Aziz aboard USS *Quincy*.
17 February. Britain's prime minister, Winston Churchill, meets King Abdul Aziz aboard USS *Quincy*.

1946 Oil production soars to 60 million barrels a year.
December. Sultana's parents marry in

Riyadh, Saudi Arabia.

1948   Radio Makkah, the first radio station in the kingdom, is opened despite fierce opposition from the Ulema (religious men). *14 May*. The state of Israel is established. The first Arab–Israeli war begins.

1952   King Abdul Aziz bans alcohol imports for non-believers.

1953   *9 November*. King Abdul Aziz, Sultana's grandfather, dies at the age of seventy-seven. His eldest son, fifty-one-year-old Sa'ud, becomes king. His half-brother Faisal becomes crown prince.

1956   Sultana is born into the family of Al Sa'ud, the tenth daughter of her parents.

1958   *March*. With the kingdom in financial turmoil, Crown Prince Faisal takes administrative control of the Government.

1960   *December*. King Sa'ud dismisses his brother from administrative duties and assumes control of the Government.

1962   Slavery is abolished in the Kingdom of Saudi Arabia. Most slaves continue to live with the families that owned them.

1963   The first girls' school opens; religious factions riot.

1964   *3 November*. King Sa'ud abdicates and leaves the kingdom for Beirut. Faisal is declared king, and his half-brother Khalid crown prince.

1965   Despite protests, the first television station is opened in Riyadh.

September. Prince Khalid ibn Musa'id, nephew of King Faisal, is killed as he leads an armed protest against the opening of the television station.

1967   *June*. The Six-Day War begins between Israel and her Arab neighbours. Saudi Arabia sends forces.

1969   *February*. Deposed ex-king Sa'ud ibn Abdul Aziz dies in Athens after spending more than $15 million each year of his exile.

1973   *6 October*. The October 1973 war begins between Israel and her Arab neighbours. Saudi Arabia sends troops.

20 October. Furious at America's military assistance to Israel, King Faisal announces a holy war and oil embargo against America.

1975   *25 March*. King Faisal is assassinated by his nephew Prince Faisal ibn Musa'id, brother of the prince who was shot and killed during a riot in 1965. Crown Prince Khalid is declared king. His half-brother Fahd is named new crown prince.

1977   King Khalid issues a government decree that forbids women from travelling outside their homes unless accompanied by a male family member. A second order follows that forbids women from travelling abroad to study. Both decrees resulted from an international incident involving Princess Misha'il, who was publicly

317

executed after meeting and falling in love with another Saudi student at the American University in Lebanon. Her lover was beheaded.

1979   *November.* The Grand Mosque in Makkah is attacked. Protesters complain of women working outside the home in the kingdom. In the months to follow, women's freedom is curtailed in response to government fear of increased fundamentalist unrest.

1982   *June.* King Khalid dies of a heart attack. Fahd, his half-brother, is declared king; his half-brother Abdullah is named new crown prince.

1990   *5 August.* Kuwait is invaded by Iraq. Western Allied forces gather in Saudi Arabia to join Arab armies in repelling Saddam's army.

1991   *Mutawas* react with fear and hostility to the presence of foreign female soldiers. Pressure increases to force the Saudi government to tighten restrictions on the female population of all nationalities as religious factions return to strict interpretation of the Koran.

THE MANSIONS OF LIMBO
by Dominick Dunne

Tina Brown, Editor-in-Chief of *Vanity Fair*, writes:–

'He is one of those writers who seem effortlessly to collide with copy. Movie stars confide to his answering machine. Wanted men hail the same taxi. Heiresses unload their life stories in elevators. Except, of course, Dunne's luck is not luck. People love to talk to him because he has a gift for intimacy that is real and generous. While he never loses his extraordinary news sense, he is not afraid to be moved.'

In **The Mansions of Limbo**, Dominick Dunne has managed to talk with some of the most fascinating people of the decade. Against all odds, the reluctant Queen Noor of Jordan finally granted him an interview in the month directly preceding the Gulf War. The former wife of the former President of the United States gave him her first interview in nine years, and a night club queen in Las Vegas told him of her long affair with a notorious mobster. Whether in a tent by Lake Geneva as the jewels of the late Duchess of Windsor are being auctioned; or in a mansion in Beverly Hills deciphering the decade's most notorious double murder case, Dunne moves easily among the famous and infamous.

As a novelist and journalist, Dominick Dunne has explored the lives of the beautiful and not-so-beautiful people. **The Mansions of Limbo** is a piercing, intimately revealing view of the private realms where they work and play – and where the usual rules of behaviour don't apply . . .

'Searing eye on the fall of the rich and famous'
Sunday Times

A Bantam Paperback

0553 40399 0

A SELECTION OF FINE TITLES
FROM BANTAM BOOKS

THE PRICES SHOWN BELOW WERE CORRECT AT THE TIME OF GOING TO PRESS. HOWEVER TRANSWORLD PUBLISHERS RESERVE THE RIGHT TO SHOW NEW RETAIL PRICES ON COVERS WHICH MAY DIFFER FROM THOSE PREVIOUSLY ADVERTISED IN THE TEXT OR ELSEWHERE.

☐ 17523 8	**THE CAT WHO CAME FOR CHRISTMAS**			
			Cleveland Amory	£4.99
☐ 40356 7	**THE CAT WHO CAME FOR CHRISTMAS 2**			
			Cleveland Amory	£4.99
☐ 40540 3	**CHILDHOOD**		*Bill Cosby*	£3.99
☐ 17463 0	**FATHERHOOD**		*Bill Cosby*	£3.50
☐ 40050 9	**LOVE AND MARRIAGE**		*Bill Cosby*	£3.50
☐ 17517 3	**TIME FLIES**		*Bill Cosby*	£2.99
☐ 40260 9	**TO SAVE AN ELEPHANT**	*Allan Thornton and Dave Currey*		£5.99
☐ 40399 0	**MANSIONS OF LIMBO**		*Dominick Dunne*	£4.99
☐ 17542 4	**THE LIVES OF JOHN LENNON**		*Albert Goldman*	£6.99
☐ 40162 9	**WINSTON AND CLEMENTINE**		*Richard Hough*	£7.99
☐ 40424 5	**NANCY REAGAN**		*Kitty Kelley*	£4.99
☐ 17245 X	**HIS WAY: THE UNAUTHORISED BIOGRAPHY**			
	OF FRANK SINATRA		*Kitty Kelley*	£3.95
☐ 40498 9	**DANCE WHILE YOU CAN**		*Shirley MacLaine*	£4.99
☐ 17239 5	**DANCING IN THE LIGHT**		*Shirley MacLaine*	£4.99
☐ 25234 8	**DON'T FALL OFF THE MOUNTAIN**		*Shirley MacLaine*	£3.99
☐ 40048 7	**GOING WITHIN**		*Shirley MacLaine*	£4.99
☐ 17512 2	**IT'S ALL IN THE PLAYING**		*Shirley MacLaine*	£4.99
☐ 17201 8	**OUT ON A LIMB**		*Shirley MacLaine*	£4.99
☐ 17364 2	**YOU CAN GET THERE FROM HERE**		*Shirley MacLaine*	£3.99
☐ 40285 4	**A SNOWFLAKE IN MY HAND**		*Samantha Mooney*	£3.99
☐ 40525 X	**NO MINOR CHORDS**		*André Previn*	£4.99
☐ 40569 1	**MARILYN AND ME**		*Susan Strasberg*	£4.99
☐ 40624 8	**THE DEATH LOBBY**	*Kenneth R. Timmerman*		£6.99
☐ 40003 7	**TRUE BLUE: THE OXFORD BOAT**			
	RACE MUTINY		*Daniel Topolski*	£4.99
☐ 40354 0	**A DIFFERENT KIND OF LIFE**		*Virginia Williams*	£4.99

All Corgi and Bantam Books are available at your bookshop or newsagent, or can be ordered from the following address:

Corgi/Bantam Books,
Cash Sales Department,
P.O. Box 11, Falmouth, Cornwall TR10 9EN

UK and B.F.P.O customers please send a cheque or postal order (no currency) and allow £1.00 for postage and packing for one book, an additional 50p for the second book, and an additional 30p for each subsequent book ordered to a maximum charge of £3.00 (7 books plus).

Overseas customers, including Eire, please allow £2.00 for postage and packing for the first book plus £1.00 for the second book and 50p for each subsequent title ordered.

Name: (Block Letters) ....

Address: ....

....